HISTORY & GEOGRAPHY 710

Social Sciences Review

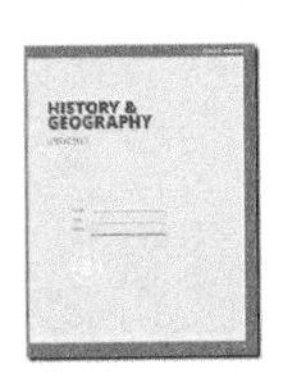

LIFEPAC Test is located in the center of the booklet. Please remove before starting the unit.

Author:
Alpha Omega Staff

Editor:
Alan Christopherson, M.S.

Westover Studios Design Team:
Phillip Pettet, Creative Lead
Teresa Davis, DTP Lead
Nick Castro
Andi Graham
Jerry Wingo

804 N. 2nd Ave. E.
Rock Rapids, IA 51246-1759

Social Sciences Review

Introduction

History is one continuous story beginning with the Father before the Creation. In fact, history can be defined as the known story of man and his relationship to God, to mankind, and to his environment. Ancient civilizations had their own sense of history, and some of their elements also are found in the Hebrew-Christian view of history today.

The character of the historian and the accuracy of his data determine the quality of historiography. The historian must possess moral standards. He must be accurate, honest, and free of prejudice.

Geography is the study of the earth's shape, movement, and relief. The geography of the earth (man's physical environment) determines, to a large extent, the way people live and the cultures they develop.

Anthropology and sociology are two social sciences directly concerned with the study of man, his way of life or culture, and his social groups and institutions. In this LIFEPAC® you will learn that the anthropologist and the sociologist must possess many of the same traits of character required of the historian.

Economics is the study of the ways man attempts to use his resources to provide for his basic needs and to fulfill some of his wants and desires. In this LIFEPAC® you will learn that the Bible teaches us, Christians, that our heavenly Father knows all our needs. You will also learn that the Bible teaches us many principles of financial responsibility.

Political science is concerned with the rules and procedures man uses to govern himself. In this LIFEPAC you will learn how Western political thought directly influenced one of our nation's most important documents, the Preamble to the Declaration of Independence

Objectives

Read these objectives. The objectives tell you what you will be able to do when you have successfully completed this LIFEPAC. When you have finished this LIFEPAC, you should be able to:

1. Define the Christian's view of history.
2. Identify the contributions of ancient civilizations.
3. Describe the elements of the historical method.
4. Give examples of the relationship between geography and man's way of life.
5. Describe the tools and methods of the anthropologist and sociologist.
6. Explain the origin and nature of culture and of social institutions.
7. Tell how culture is influenced by environment.
8. List elements of social change.
9. Describe different economic systems.
10. Explain the origin of Western political thought.
11. Define important political and economic concepts.
12. Describe the political structure of the federal and state governments.

Survey the LIFEPAC. Ask yourself some questions about this study and write your questions here.

1. HISTORY AND GEOGRAPHY

History is one continuous story beginning with the Father before Creation. History may be defined as the known story of man and his relationship to God, to mankind, and to his environment. To Christians, history is the record of man's creation and fall, Christ's redemption for sin, and God's provision for man's eternal existence.

A complete view of history will include the political, social, economic, cultural, technological, racial, and religious aspects of man. You must study the history of all mankind to understand fully the history of any particular civilization or country.

The character of the historian and the accuracy of his **data** determine the quality of a historical account. Historical data may include both archeological remains and written records.

Geography is the study of the earth's shape, movement, and relief. To a large extent, the geography of the earth determines the way people live. The geography of the United States has helped to determine the history, growth, and development of the country.

In this section of the LIFEPAC, you will learn about the Christian view of history and the contributions of ancient cultures to **historiography**. You will learn how the historian gathers his material. You will also learn the relationship between history and geography.

SECTION OBJECTIVES

Review these objectives. When you have completed this section, you should be able to:

1. Define the Christian's view of history.
2. Identify the contributions of ancient civilizations.
3. Describe the elements of the historical method.
4. Give examples of the relationship between geography and man's way of life.

VOCABULARY

Study these words to enhance your learning success in this section.

alluvial (u lü' vi ul). Formed by sand or mud left by flowing water.

archives (är' kīvz). Place where public records or historical documents are kept.

axis (ak' sis). Straight lines about which a geometric figure rotates.

basin (bā ' sun). The land drained by a river.

contiguous (kun tig' yu us). Adjoining or touching.

continuity (kon' tu nü' u tēi). Uninterrupted; unbroken series.

cyclical (sī' klu kul). Moving or occurring in cycles.

data (dā' tu). Facts from which conclusions can be drawn.

delta (del' tu). Triangular piece of land made by deposits of mud and sand at the mouth of a river.

distributaries (dis trib' yu ter' ēz). River branches flowing away from the main stream.

equator (i kwā' tur). Imaginary circle around the middle of the earth.

equinox (ēi' kwu noks). When the sun's center crosses the equator and day and night are of equal length everywhere.

estuary (es' chü er ēi). Broad mouth of a river into which the tide flows.

foci (fō ' sī). Plural of focus; central or meeting points.

glacier (glā ' shur). A large body of ice moving slowly down a slope.

habitat (hab' u tat). Place of living; dwelling place.

historiography (his tôr ē og' ru fēi). Historical writing based on critical methods.

linear (lin' ē i ur). In a straight line.

Pilgrims (pil' grumz). People who came from England to the New World for religious reasons.

predecessors (pred' u ses urz). Ancestors or forefathers.

solstice (sol' stis). Time of year when the sun is farthest north or farthest south of the equator.

sphere (sfēir). Globe; round or ball-shaped object.

Note: *All vocabulary words in this LIFEPAC appear in* **boldface** *print the first time they are used. If you are not sure of the meaning when you are reading, study the definitions given.*

Pronunciation Key: h**a**t, **ā**ge, c**ã**re, f**ä**r; l**e**t, **ē**qual, t**ė**rm; **i**t, **ī**ce; h**o**t, **ō**pen, **ô**rder; **oi**l; **ou**t; c**u**p, p**u̇**t, r**ü**le; **ch**ild; lo**ng**; **th**in; /ŦH/ for **th**en; /zh/ for mea**s**ure; /u/ or /ə/ represents /a/ in **a**bout, /e/ in tak**e**n, /i/ in penc**i**l, /o/ in lem**o**n, and /u/ in circ**u**s.

THE MEANING OF HISTORY

A clear meaning of history is necessary if one is to make sense out of human events. A proper view of history shows the unity and continuity of these events and provides answers to man's problems. The meaning of history is derived from the definition, significance, and sense of history. Because these elements vary, the meaning of history will vary among scholars.

The definition of history. History can be defined as the past or as everything that has happened. It can also be defined as a record based on surviving or known evidence. Some individuals would define history as the writings of historians concerning important human activities. However, *history* is properly defined as *the known story of man and his relationship to God, to mankind, and to his environment.* A complete view of history will include the political, social, economic, cultural, technological, racial, and religious aspects of man.

The significance of history. History has order and meaning; it is the sum of the events that have led to the present time. The past is linked to the present and to the future. If you do not study the past, you will not be able to understand properly the present and the future. You will gain these beneficial insights from studying history:

1. Many of the contributions of ancient civilizations remain in use today. The Babylonians (1000–583 BC) have contributed ideas about law, writing, trading, and farming. They have also provided a calendar and a system of weights and measures. The Phoenicians (3000–538 BC) contributed an alphabet and the spreading of civilization to other lands. The Egyptians (2700–1090 BC) contributed a calendar, irrigation, works of art, law, astronomy, mathematics, schools, boats,

embalming, and writing. The Hebrews (2000–933 BC) contributed information about the one true God and the Old Testament literature and commandments.

2. The nature of man is constant. The Bible says (Ecclesiastes 1:9), "...There is no new thing under the sun." The nature of man does not change. Man is as sinful today as Adam was in the Fall. The only hope for sinful man is to be made new. Second Corinthians 5:17 says, "...If any man be in Christ, he is a new creature: old things are passed away; behold, all things are become new."
3. History has unity and continuity. History is one continuous story beginning with the Father before Creation. It is like a river in which the water that has come down from distant mountains mingles with the water that each new branch pours in. The continuity of history means it is one continuous story, and if it is not studied from its source, including the Father before Creation, then we will not have a proper viewpoint of man's story. You must study the history of all mankind to fully understand the history of any particular civilization or country. We are the heirs of our **predecessors**; our inheritance consists of ideas, institutions, and knowledge. However, the predecessors of one civilization may not be identical with those of another civilization. One group may be in the atomic age, and another may be in the stone age.
4. Man has conflicts. Man is engaged in three areas of conflict: spiritual, human, and natural. Spiritual conflicts involve man against the world, the flesh, and Satanic forces. Human conflicts involve man against his fellow man. Natural conflicts involve man against the forces of nature. Natural conflicts resulted from the Fall and act as a type of barometer of man's spiritual well-being. The more man submits to God's authority, the more he is able to subdue the earth.

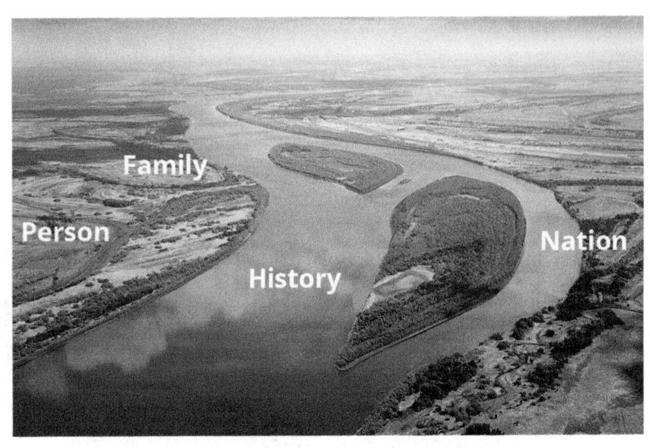

| Human history is like a river.

5. God blesses those who depend on Him. The Bible says in Romans 8:28, "...All things work together for good to them that love God...." The Scriptures contain the accounts of the lives of those that love God—people such as Noah, Moses, Joshua, Elijah, Daniel, Paul, and others. These individuals loved and depended on God and He blessed their lives. You can depend on God and be blessed by Him in your life.

The sense of history. Both the Greeks and the Hebrews had a sense of history. The Greek sense of history was **cyclical** and was developed in the sixth century before Christ. They saw nations rise and then fall and concluded that this pattern would forever repeat itself. This view of history means that no events would be unique or new. The problem with the Greek view of history is that it was limited. They viewed history from the way it was happening then, concluding that it had no purpose. What the Greeks lacked for a proper view of history was the right point of view and a total picture of the course of human events. Both of these elements are found in the Hebrew-Christian view of history.

| Cyclical View of History

The Hebrews believed history was the story of man's ultimate purpose as he related to God. To Christians, history is the record of man's creation and fall, Christ's redemption for sin, and God's provision for man's eternal existence. This view of history is called **linear** history because it has a beginning and an ultimate end. The total picture of history can be found in the Bible, the record from Creation to judgment and eternity.

The most common division of history uses the birth of Christ as the focal point. Times before His birth are called BC (before Christ), while times afterwards are called AD (Anno Domini). Modern humanists are trying to remove Christ from history. They use the term CE (Common Era) and BCE (Before Common Era) as substitutes; however, they are still divided by the birth of Christ.

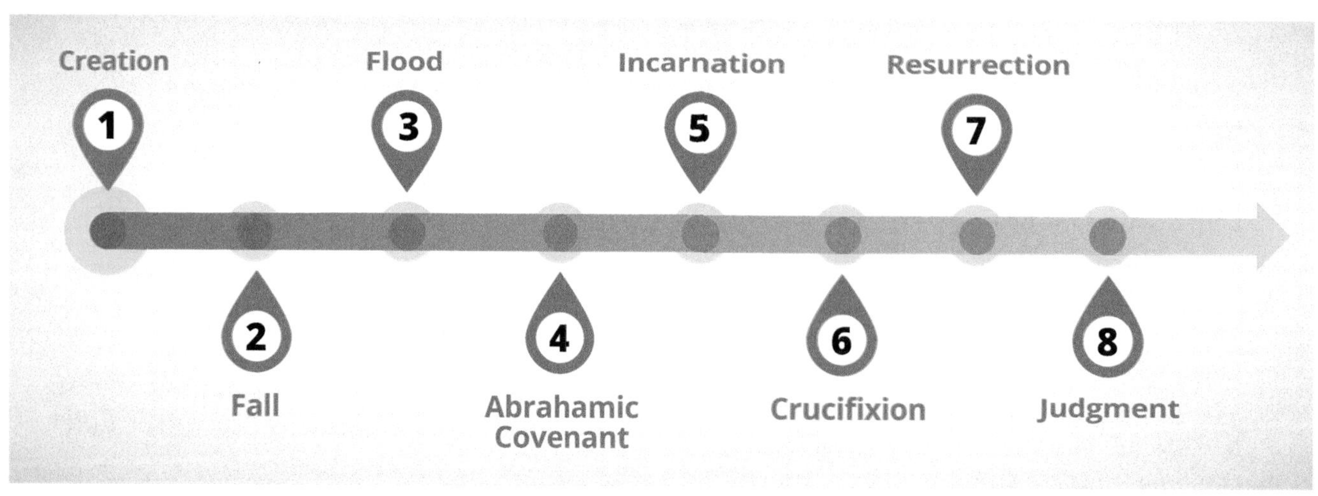

| Linear View of History

Complete the crossword.

1.1 ACROSS

1. Historical writing based on critical methods.
2. When the sun's center crosses the equator and day and night are of equal length everywhere.
3. Globe; round or ball-shaped object.
4. Ancestors or forefathers.

DOWN

1. Place of living; dwelling place.
2. Time of year when the sun is farthest north or farthest south of the equator.
3. A large body of ice moving slowly down a slope.
4. People who came from England to the New World for religious reasons.
5. Plural of focus; central or meeting points.
6. Broad mouth of a river into which the tide flows.
7. In a straight line.

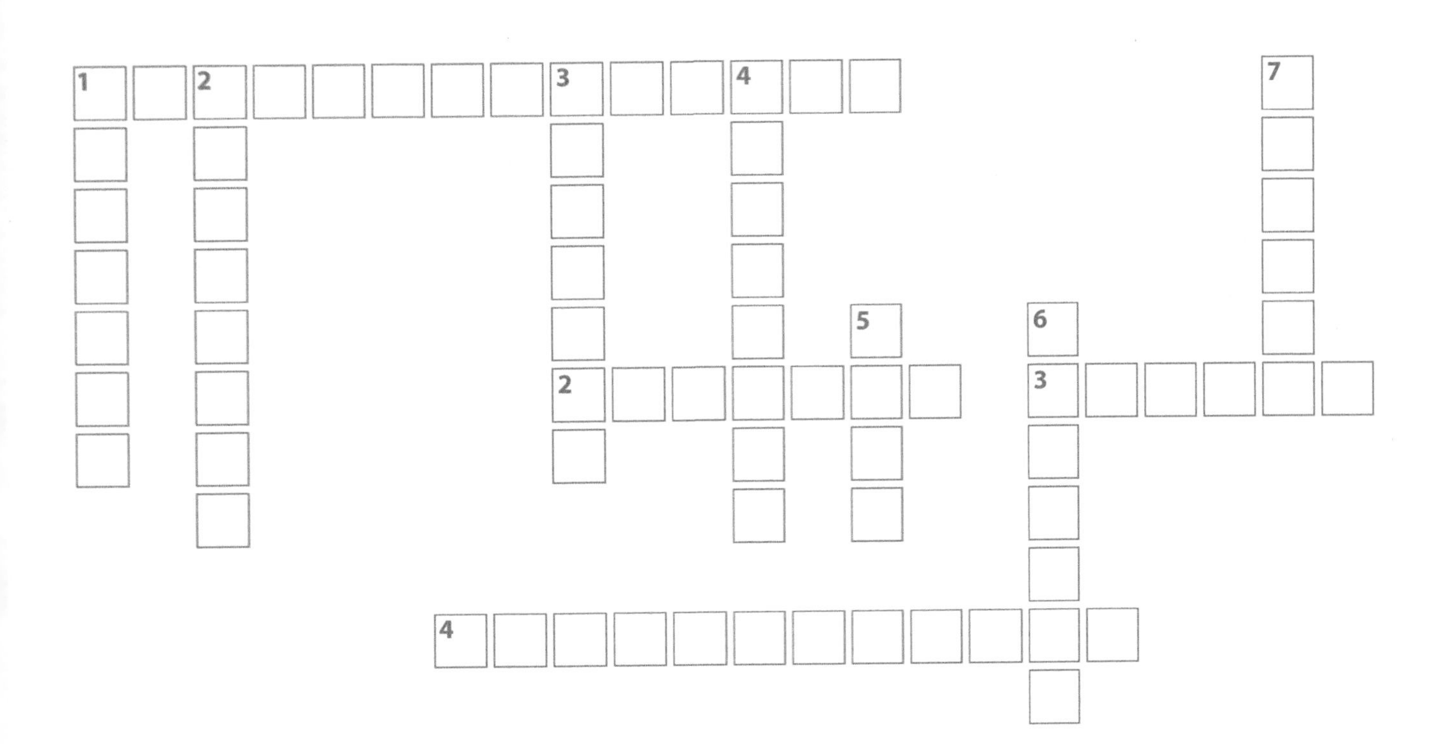

Match these vocabulary words with their definitions.

1.2 ________ alluvial
1.3 ________ archives
1.4 ________ axis
1.5 ________ basin
1.6 ________ contiguous
1.7 ________ continuity
1.8 ________ cyclical
1.9 ________ data
1.10 ________ delta
1.11 ________ distributaries
1.12 ________ equator

a. imaginary circle around the middle of the earth
b. formed by sand or mud left by flowing water
c. river branches flowing away from the main stream
d. a place where public records or historical documents are kept
e. triangular piece of land made by deposits of mud and sand at the mouth of a river
f. straight lines about which a geometric figure rotates
g. facts from which conclusions can be drawn
h. the land drained by a river
i. moving or occurring in cycles
j. adjoining or touching
k. uninterrupted; unbroken series

Complete these statements.

1.13 History is the known story of man and his relationship to a. ________________,
to b. ________________, and to c. ________________________.

1.14 A complete view of history will include several aspects of man, including
a. ________________________, b. ________________________, and
c. ________________________.

1.15 Among the contributions of the ancient Babylonians were a. ________________________,
b. ________________________, and c. ________________________.

1.16 Phoenicians contributed a. ________________ and b. ________________________.

1.17 The Hebrews contributed a. ________________________________ and
b. ____.

1.18 The Greek sense of history was ________________ ; they believed the pattern of history would forever repeat itself.

1.19 The Hebrew sense of history was ________________ ; they believed history had a beginning and an end.

1.20 The Bible provides the total picture of history from a. ________________ to b. ________________ and eternity.

Write *true* or *false*.

1.21 ____________ The nature of man is constantly changing.

1.22 ____________ Modern man is as sinful today as Adam was in the Fall.

1.23 ____________ History began with the Father before Creation.

1.24 ____________ To fully understand the history of any one civilization or country, you must study the history of all mankind.

1.25 ____________ Predecessors of all civilizations are identical.

1.26 ____________ Man is engaged in three areas of conflict: spiritual, human, and natural.

THE HISTORICAL METHOD

Two primary elements determine the quality of a historical account: the historian and the **data** he uses. The historian must possess certain characteristics for his history to be accepted. The data used in the history must be treated carefully and purposefully to be useful.

The historian. Historians must have certain qualities of character. Of primary importance is the quality of accuracy. If the historian is not accurate, his writing cannot be relied upon. The historian must also be patient, tenacious, moral, and honest. A very difficult task for a historian is to overcome prejudice. He must erase from his mind any preconceived notions as to how something happened.

The historian must be imaginative. He must be able to imagine what happened based on the facts he has gathered. Because not all of the facts can ever be discovered, the historian must re-create some events that he believes probably happened. In gathering the facts, he must be versatile and skillful in many areas of research. Finally, the historian must be judgmental. He must take a position concerning the past and must communicate that position in his **historiography**.

The data. The evidence that the historian uses in historiography is called data. Data come from two sources: primary sources and secondary sources. A primary source is information from the same period as the subject being studied. A secondary source is information from a later period concerning the one under study. Libraries mostly have more secondary sources, the analysis and interpretations of other authors. Archaeological sites, museums, and **archives** usually have more primary sources than secondary.

Data is divided into two categories: archaeological remains and written records.

Archaeological remains may include: (1) material remains such as bones, tools, weapons, and pottery; (2) oral traditions such as poetry, myths, legends, and songs; and (3) pictorial data such as drawings and maps.

Written records may include ancient manuscripts, treaties, diaries, books, magazines, and newspapers.

Dating the primary data is often a difficult task. Although many techniques exist for dating prehistoric material, none of them is absolutely precise. Most dating methods depend on measurements of change. For example, the salinity of the sea increases with time; the layers of sedimentation become thicker with time; the radioactivity in rock and other material decreases with time. The age of something is said to be related to how much it has changed. However, dating by measuring the amount of change in something is unreliable for two reasons. First, unless the material has been measured at the beginning of the time period, you cannot know how much it has changed to the present. Second, the rate of change of any material is not constant. Therefore, the dates assigned to the earth and its prehistoric archaeological remains should be considered as estimates only.

When the historian tests the genuineness of his data, he must decide if it is accurate, authentic, complete, and reliable. He tests his data against other data, against "outside information," to determine their genuineness. If he is testing written documents, he must also examine "inside information." The meaning and accuracy of a document is determined by studying its language, the integrity of its author, and its correspondence with reliable evidence on the same subject. After the genuineness of his data has been determined, the author tries to present the facts as they happened.

Write *true* or *false*.

1.27 ____________ Many absolute techniques exist for dating prehistoric material.

1.28 ____________ The historian must test his data against both outside and inside information.

1.29 ____________ The historian must sometimes use his imagination to help tell the story of the past.

1.30 ____________ Libraries usually contain only primary sources.

1.31 ____________ Dates assigned to the earth and to its prehistoric remains are only estimates.

1.32 ____________ Prehistoric material changes at a constant and predictable rate.

1.33 ____________ The principal elements that determine the quality of an historical account are the character of the historian and the accuracy of his data.

Complete these statements.

1.34 Information from the same period as the subject is a _______________ source of historical data.

1.35 Information from a later period concerning the period being studied is called a _______________ source.

1.36 Historical data are divided into two categories: a. _______________ remains and b. _______________ records.

1.37 Historians must be characterized as being a. _______________, b. _______________, c. _______________, d. _______________, and e. _______________.

1.38 Written records that are valuable to historians include a. _______________, b. _______________, c. _______________, and d. _______________.

THE GEOGRAPHY OF THE EARTH

Geography is the study of the earth's surface, climate, continents, countries, people, industries, and products. The geography of the earth largely determines the way we live. Geography can be divided into several classes:

1. **Physical geography**: the study of the physical features of the earth and their effect on man.
2. **Meteorology**: the study of the earth's atmosphere.
3. **Climatology**: the study of average weather.
4. **Economic geography**: the study of man's economic activities over the earth's surface.
5. **Urban geography**: the study of the life of cities.
6. **Political geography**: the study of the relation of the landforms to governments.

| Geography is the study of the earth.

7. **Mathematical geography**: a study of the measurements of the earth.
8. **Cultural geography**: the study of the geographic distribution of cultures.
9. **Regional geography**: the study of a region by using geographic principles.

Much of the earth's geography is a product of the earth itself and its relationship to the sun. The shape, movement, and relief of the earth are primary elements in geography.

The shape of the earth. The earth is an imperfect **sphere**; it is slightly flattened at the poles, and it bulges slightly at the **equator**. The diameter of the earth is approximately 7,927 miles at the equator; the diameter between the poles is 1/297 less.

As seen from space, the surface of the earth appears to be relatively smooth. However, mountains and ocean depths make the surface uneven. The highest point on the earth is the top of Mount Everest, 29,028 feet above sea level. The deepest point on the earth's surface is in the Mariana Trench, 35,800 feet below sea level. The difference between the highest and lowest points on the earth's surface is slightly more than twelve miles.

Because the shape of the earth is spherical, it is difficult to portray on a flat map. Three of the most important map projections are the polar projection, the interrupted area projection, and the Mercator projection. The polar projection usually shows the North Pole and the land in the Northern Hemisphere. This type of map is often used to indicate great circle routes for airplanes. A great circle is a line, such as the equator, that divides the earth into two equal parts. The interrupted area projection has blank spaces between the continents so that the continents can be displayed flat with little distortion. The Mercator projection is especially useful in determining direction, because it is a rectangular, flat projection of the earth.

Locating any point of the earth's surface is done by referring to the longitude and latitude of that point. The lines of longitude are vertical, and the lines of latitude are horizontal on the map. Lines of longitude are called meridians and extend from the North Pole to the South Pole. Each of the 360 meridians corresponds to a degree measured from the prime meridian (0°). The prime meridian runs through Greenwich, England; 180 meridians lie to the east of the prime meridian; and 180 meridians lie to the west.

Lines of latitude are called parallels and extend east and west parallel with the equator. Each of the 180 parallels corresponds to a degree measured from the equator (0°). To the north of the equator lie 90 parallels, and to the south lie 90 parallels. The distance between parallels can be divided into 60 minutes, and the distance between minutes can be divided into 60 seconds. The distance between seconds is about thirty-five meters; the distance between minutes is slightly more than one nautical mile; the distance between parallels is sixty-nine nautical miles. At the equator the distance between meridians is also sixty-nine nautical miles, but the distance is reduced to zero at the poles.

The movement of the earth. The earth makes one complete rotation every twenty-four hours. This movement produces the periods of light and darkness over most of the earth. However, at the North Pole the sun never completely sets during the summer months and never rises over the horizon during the winter months.

The condition of prolonged light and darkness at the poles results from the tilted **axis** of the earth. As the earth makes its 365¼ day trip around the sun, its axis does not change position; the North Pole always points toward the North Star. The axis of the earth is tilted 23½ degrees from being perpendicular to its orbit. The tilted axis also produces the winter and summer **solstices**. The winter solstice occurs on December 21, and the summer

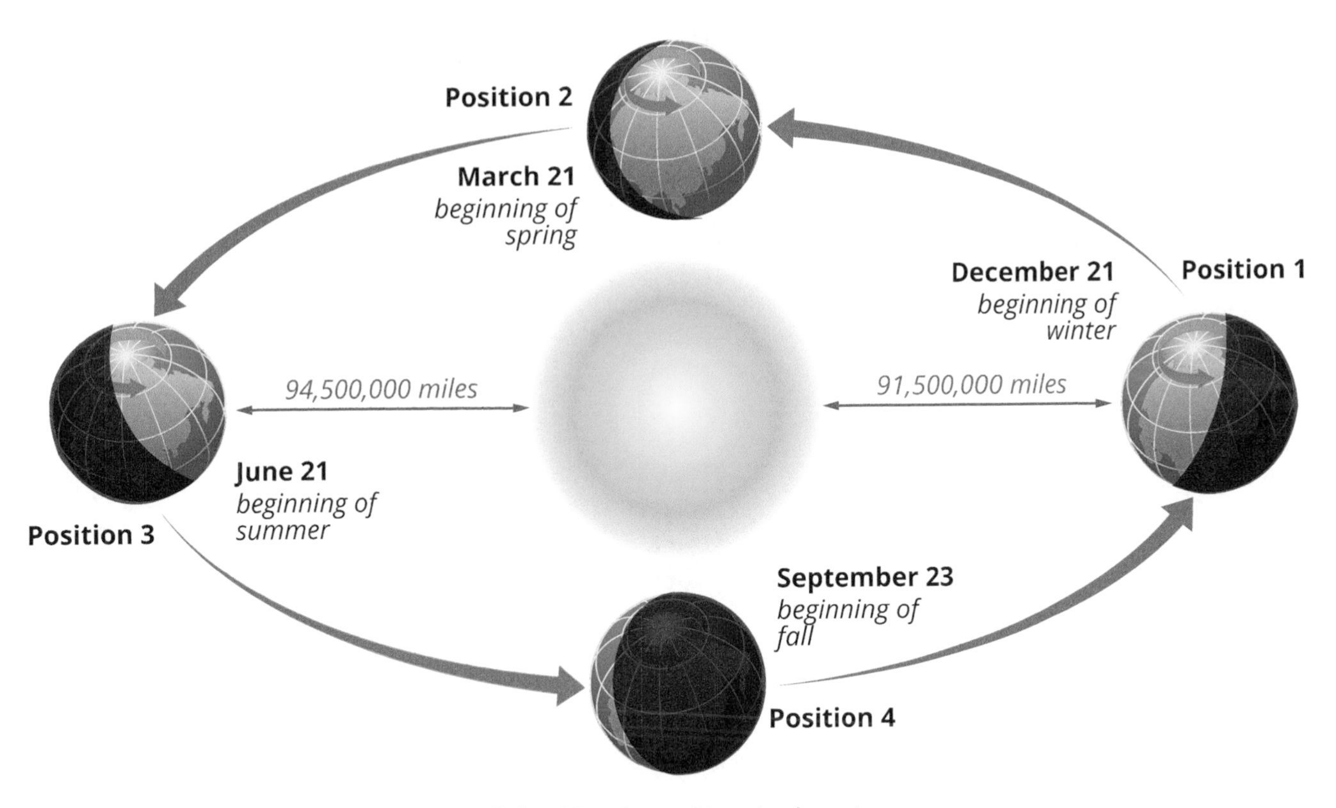

| Positions of the Earth (Seasons of the Northern Hemisphere)

solstice occurs six months later on June 21. At the winter solstice the most direct rays of the sun strike the earth along a line 23½ degrees south of the equator, the Tropic of Capricorn. During this time the sun does not shine on the area bounded by the Arctic Circle and it shines continually on the area bounded by the Antarctic Circle. The Arctic Circle is 23½ degrees south of the North Pole, and the Antarctic Circle is 23½ degrees north of the South Pole. At the summer solstice the most direct rays of the sun strike the earth along a line 23½ degrees north of the equator, the Tropic of Cancer. The conditions of light and darkness at the poles during this time are opposite from those of the winter solstice.

Midway between the solstices are the **equinoxes**. At an "equinox" every place on earth will have an "equal night" twelve hours long. The most direct rays of the sun will fall in the equator. The vernal (spring) equinox occurs on March 21, and the autumnal equinox occurs on September 23.

The earth turns on its axis from west to east. It turns through 15 degrees of longitude every hour, 360 degrees every twenty-four hours. Twenty-four time zones have been established for the world. Each time zone is 15 degrees

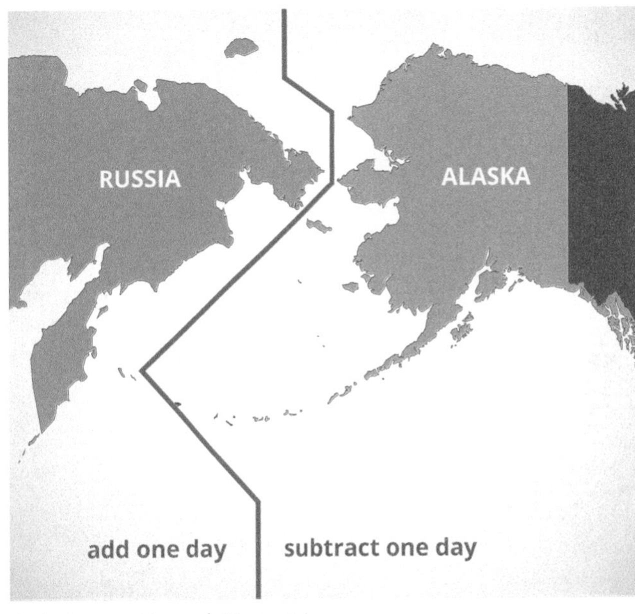

| International Date Line

wide and represents a time of one hour. The time at any point in a time zone will be one hour later than in the zone to the west and one hour earlier than in the zone to the east. The **contiguous** states of the United States have four time zones: Pacific, Mountain, Central, and Eastern. Alaska has three time zones: Bering, Alaska-Hawaii, and Yukon. Most of Alaska and all of Hawaii are in the Alaska-Hawaii time zone.

The 180th meridian is the International Date Line. The International Date Line serves as the boundary of the twenty-four time zones. If an individual crossed this boundary traveling westward, he would gain one day; if he crossed it traveling eastward, he would lose one day. For instance, if he began to cross it Tuesday noon, he would cross into Wednesday noon going westward and into Monday noon going eastward.

Complete these statements.

1.39 The study of the features of the earth and their effect on man is called ______________________ geography.

1.40 The study of the earth's atmosphere is a. ______________________ ; the study of average weather is b. ______________________ .

1.41 The earth makes one complete rotation every ______________________ hours.

1.42 Lines of latitude extend a. ______________ and b. ______________ .

1.43 Lines of longitude extend from the a. ______________ to the b. ______________ .

1.44 Each of the world's a. ______________________ time zones represents one b. ______________ of time.

Match the following.

1.45 ________ vernal equinox

1.46 ________ North Pole

1.47 ________ winter solstice

1.48 ________ longitude

1.49 ________ autumnal equinox

1.50 ________ prime meridian

1.51 ________ South Pole

1.52 ________ lowest point on earth

1.53 ________ latitude

1.54 ________ 180th meridian

a. Greenwich, England
b. Mariana Trench
c. March 21
d. International Date Line
e. Arctic
f. Antarctic
g. meridians
h. Mount Everest
i. September 23
j. June 21
k. parallels
l. December 21

Complete these statements.

1.55 Geography includes the study of a. ______________________________, b. ______________________________, c. ______________________________, and d. ______________________________.

1.56 Three of the most important map projections are the a. ______________________________, b. ______________________________, and c. ______________________________.

1.57 The four times zones of the contiguous states are a. ______________________________, b. ______________________________, c. ______________________________, and d. ______________________________.

Write *true* or *false*.

1.58 ______________ The geography of the earth largely determines the way people live.

1.59 ______________ Much of the earth's geography is a product of the earth itself and its relationship to the sun.

1.60 ______________ The earth is a perfect sphere with a smooth, even surface.

1.61 ______________ Because the shape of the earth is spherical, it can be easily portrayed on a flat map.

1.62 ______________ The Mercator projection, using lines of longitude and latitude, is helpful in determining directions.

1.63 ______________ Great circle routes indicated by polar projections are commonly used for airplanes.

1.64 ______________ At an equinox, every place on earth will have an equal night of twelve hours long.

1.65 ______________ Conditions of prolonged light and darkness at the poles result from strong ocean tides.

The relief of the earth. A relief is a geographical feature of the earth. Reliefs include mountains, plateaus, hills, plains, rivers and valleys, **deltas**, and oceans and seas.

Rivers usually begin high on a mountain. The water coming from a spring or a **glacier** is swift as it moves down the mountainside. The river moves through a valley, enlarging it along the way. Tributaries from several valleys join to make a deep, wide river. As the river flows off the mountain and away from the hills, it is no longer contained by rocky walls. It makes its own deep, wide bed on a plain. On the plain a river moves slowly, meandering as it goes. As it approaches the sea, a river can open into an **estuary** or a delta and join the sea. A delta is formed when **distributaries** leave the river to join the sea. Deltas occur on the Mississippi, the Nile, and the Ganges rivers.

About 70 percent of the earth's surface is covered by water. Most of the water lies in the Atlantic, Pacific, Indian, and Arctic oceans. The seas are areas of ocean partly surrounded by land.

Oceans affect man in several ways. They separate land masses, providing natural barriers to invaders. The waters above the continental shelf, a belt of land lying along the margins of the continents, provide many nations with fish. The continental shelf is not deeper than six hundred feet below the water's surface and contains minerals such as oil and coal. The oceans and seas also affect the climate of the lands. Coastal areas are cooled by breezes coming in across the water in summer and are heated by the breezes in winter. Warm ocean currents, such as the Gulf Stream or the North Atlantic Drift, keep ports and harbors free of ice in the winter. Cold ocean currents, such as the Labrador Current, help ice to form in the harbors.

Mountains are high, rugged areas of land. Their slopes are often steep, and their climate is severe. Some mountains are high enough

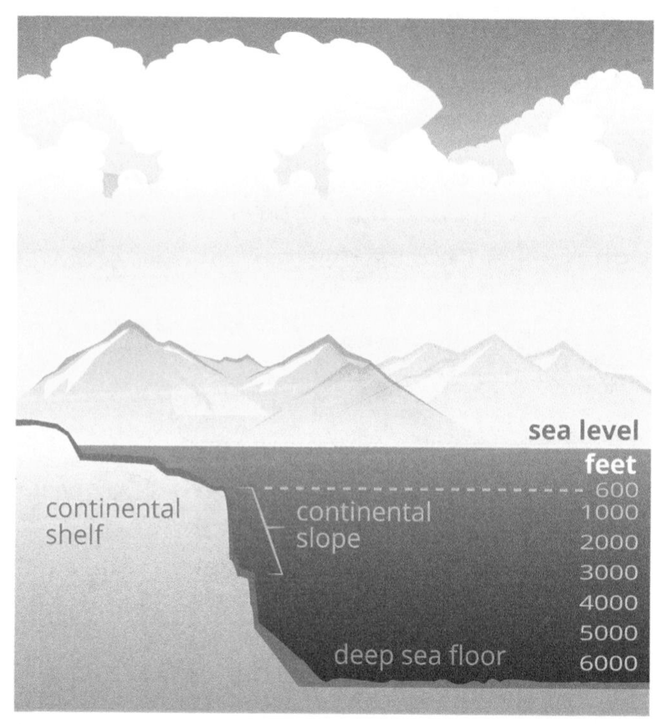

| Continental Shelf

to have a snowcap throughout the year. This snow is the result of the vertical climate of the mountains. For every 300 feet in elevation, the temperature drops one degree.

Mountains are barriers; they prevent transportation, rainfall, and farming. Some mountains are so high and rugged that people can cross them only through the passes or through a tunnel. High mountains also prevent moisture-laden winds from crossing. As a consequence, deserts are formed (such as parts of Nevada to the east of the Sierra Nevadas). Because the soil is too thin, mountains support little agriculture.

Mountainous regions do provide for many occupations. Sheep and goats are raised in the rugged mountains of New Zealand and Europe. Mining is important in mountain areas because minerals, such as gold, silver, copper, and coal, are close to the surface. The cool temperatures and abundant rainfall are ideal for tall trees and make lumbering an important mountain industry.

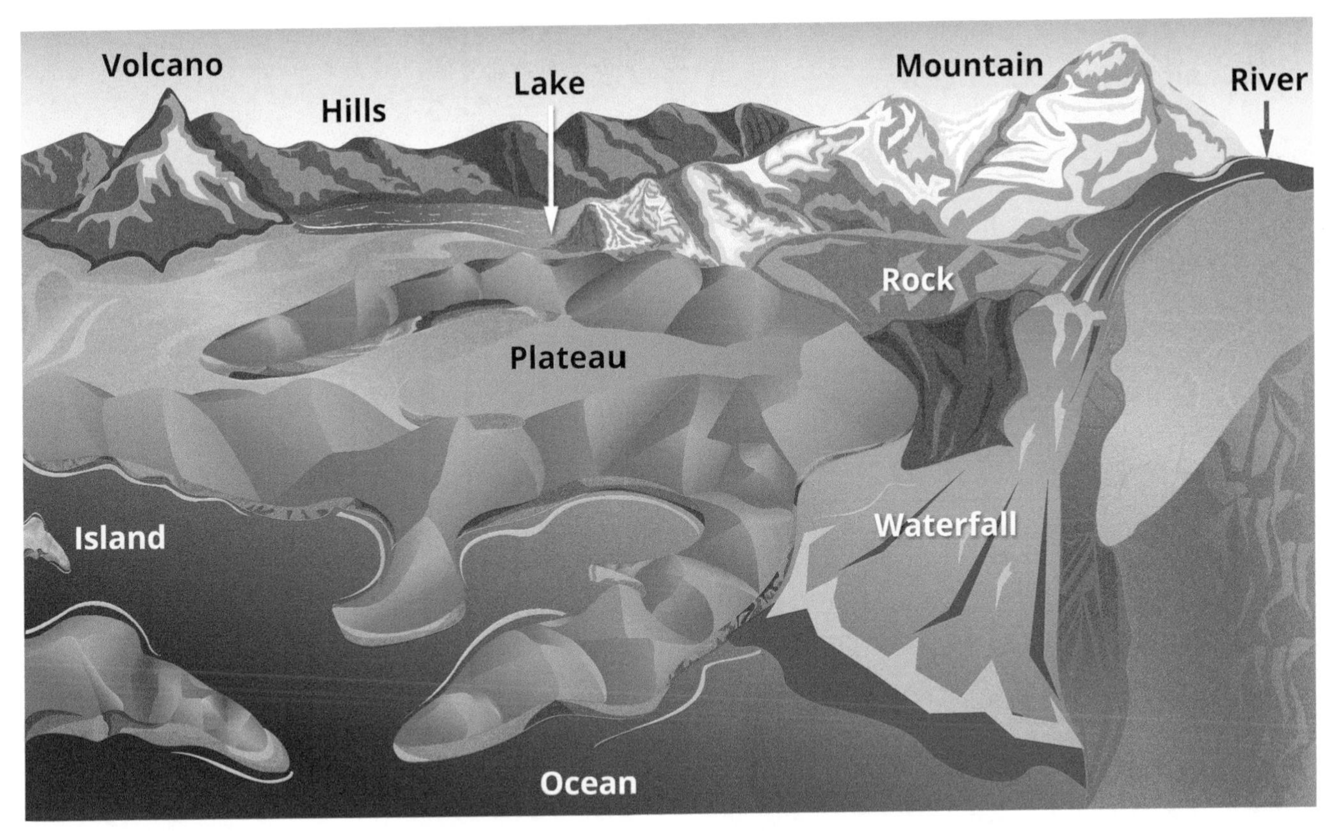

| Landforms

A plateau is a high, flat area of land. It resembles a plain, but it is cooler and more easily drained. The soil on a plateau will not support much farming but is usually very good as grazing land. The high sides of the plateau cause winds to lose their moisture before blowing across the surface of the land; rainfall is then scarce or uncertain on the plateau. Steep cliffs also hinder transportation between the plateau and the lower plains.

Hills are irregular levels of land and present many difficulties for farming and transportation. The soil on many hills is rocky; and, where it can be plowed, much of it is often washed down into the valleys. Roads among hills are expensive to construct. Steep slopes must be cut and bridges must be built to make the winding road as straight and level as possible.

Plains are vast expanses of relatively flat land. The soil on many plains is deep and fertile and supports most of the world's farming. In some areas the fertility of the soil is maintained by the **alluvial** deposits laid down by the periodic flooding of a river. The plains along the Nile River in Egypt, the "Gift of the Nile," are kept fertile by the yearly flooding of the river.

Most of the great population centers are on plains. Level land makes transportation by road, rail, and river very easy. With good transportation comes manufacturing and trade centers, the **foci** of population.

The three major plains areas in the world are the North American Plains, the Eurasian Plains, and the Amazon **Basin**. The first two of these lowland areas constitute extensive agricultural areas. The Amazon Basin is primarily rain forest drained by the Amazon River. This river is navigable by large ships for almost one thousand miles.

Complete these activities.

1.66 Reliefs, or geological features of the earth, include a. ________________,
b. ________________, c. ________________, and d. ________________.

1.67 Define these terms.

a. delta ____

____

b. seas ____

____

c. plains ____

____

d. plateau ____

____

Complete these statements.

1.68 Almost ________________ percent of the earth's surface is covered by water.

1.69 Deltas occur on the a. ________________ River in the United States, the
b. ________________ River in Egypt, and the c. ________________ River in India.

1.70 Three occupations typical of mountainous regions that were mentioned in the text are
a. ________________, b. ________________, and c. ________________.

1.71 Three major plains areas in the world are the a. ________________ Plains, the
b. ________________ Plains, and the c. ________________ Basin.

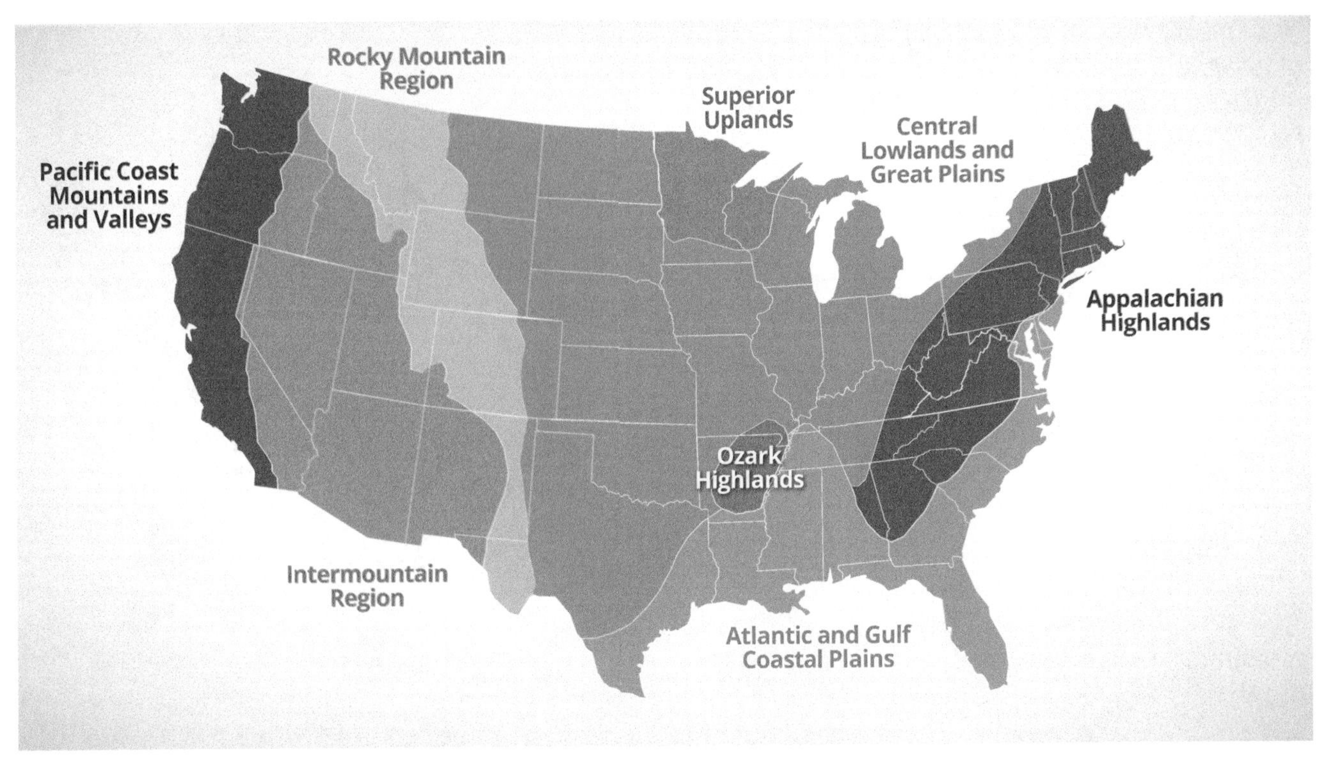

| Landform Regions of the United States

THE GEOGRAPHY AND EARLY HISTORY OF THE UNITED STATES

The United States is a nation of fifty states. Forty-nine states lie on the North American continent, and one state (Hawaii) lies in the Pacific Ocean. Before European explorers came to North America, the land was settled by many groups of Native Americans. These groups differed from each other in language, **habitat**, and culture.

Europeans began exploring parts of North America more than nine hundred years ago. Although most of the explorers were looking for wealth rather than for a new home, the lands they found and claimed were soon settled by European immigrants. The settlement of the forty-eight contiguous states varied from region to region. The landforms, climate, and resources greatly affected the early history of the United States.

The Northeast. The Northeast was first explored by the Vikings of Norway about AD 1000. In 1609 Henry Hudson sailed up the Hudson River and claimed that area for Holland. He named it New Holland. It is the area that is now known as New York City. The first permanent European settlement in the

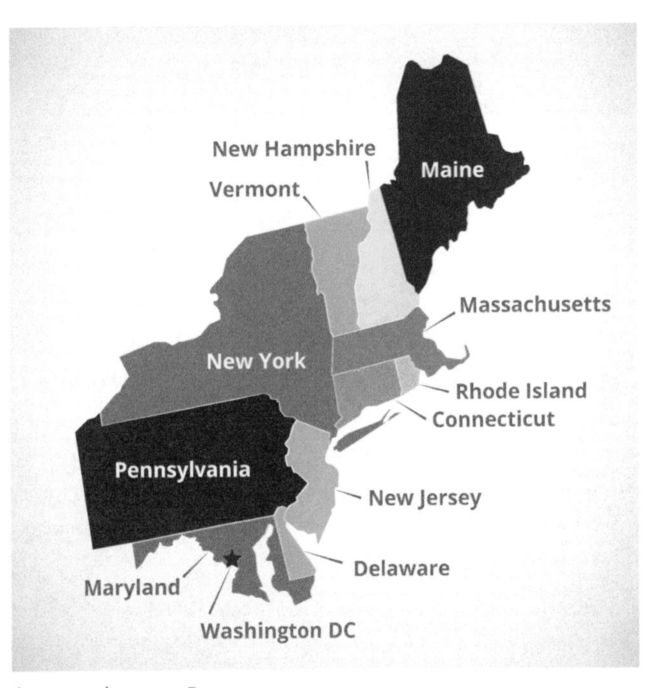

| Northeast States

Northeast was established in 1620 at Plymouth, Massachusetts. These early settlers were called **Pilgrims**; they had come from Europe to the New World to gain religious freedom.

The states in the Northeast are Connecticut, Delaware, Maine, Maryland, Massachusetts, New Hampshire, New Jersey, New York, Pennsylvania, Rhode Island, and Vermont. Washington, D.C. is also considered a part of this region.

The landforms of the Northeast include the Atlantic Coastal Plain, the Appalachian Highlands, and other lowlands. Along the coastline are many bays and inlets where a prosperous fishing industry exists. The coastal plain supports many truck farms and dairies. It has a milder climate than the highlands, but the growing season is no longer than about seven months.

The highlands do not support much agriculture because of the thin, rocky soil and the short growing season. The climate in the highlands is usually severe, having heavy winter snowfalls. Highland industries include wood pulp, mining, quarrying, and growing Christmas trees. The wood pulp is made into paper used by the Northeastern publishers. This region has one of the world's largest publishing industries.

The lowland areas produce many agricultural crops. These crops include grapes, apples, potatoes, cranberries, peaches, and vegetables. The climate in the lowlands is not as warm as that of the coastal plain nor as cold as that of the highlands.

The Northeast was the scene of two revolutions: the Revolutionary War and the Industrial Revolution. Because the Northeast has many rivers and waterfalls to power machinery, it became the center of industry in the United States. The Industrial Revolution began in the Northeast where the factories were located. Urbanization also began in this region; the factories needed many workers. One of the first factories in this region was the spinning mill built by Samuel Slater in 1789.

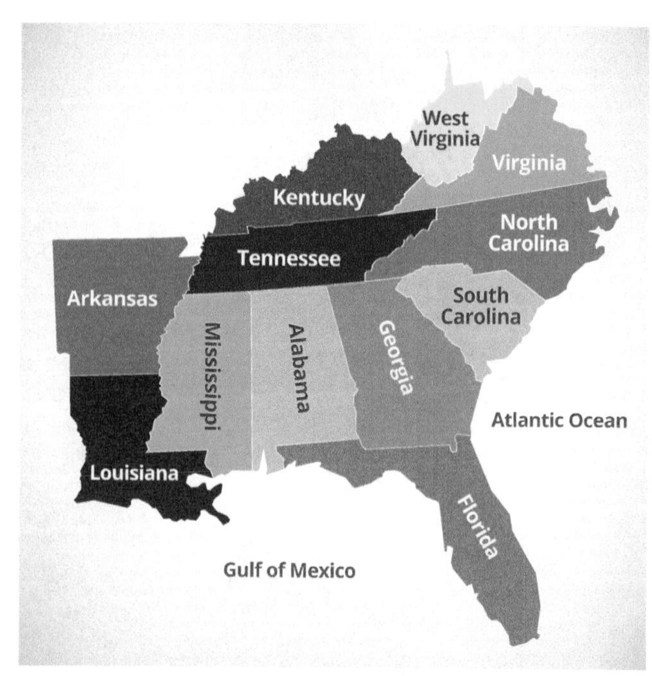

| Southern States

The South. The Spanish were the first to explore and to claim much of the South. Ponce de León landed on the Florida peninsula in 1513; and in 1539, Hernando de Soto explored and claimed the land from Florida to the Mississippi River for Spain. The first European settlement in the South was established by the Spanish in St. Augustine, Florida in 1565.

The states in the South are Alabama, Arkansas, Florida, Georgia, Kentucky, Louisiana, Mississippi, North Carolina, South Carolina, Tennessee, Virginia, and West Virginia.

The landforms in the South include the Atlantic and the Gulf coastal plains, the Appalachian and the Ozark highlands, and the interior plains and lowlands. More than half of the South lies in the coastal plains. The coastal plains support much agriculture.

The Piedmont Plateau is a rocky shelf in the Appalachian Highlands. Rivers flowing off this shelf formed waterfalls where they wore away the sandy plain soil at the edge of the shelf. Pioneers traveling on rivers throughout the South were stopped at these waterfalls. The cities they established next to the waterfalls are called fall line cities.

Because the South is closer to the equator and is lower in altitude than the Northeast, it has a warmer climate than the Northeast. The South has more rainfall than any of the other regions. Consequently, the South has high humidity.

The highlands produce timber and wood products, stone, and coal, and other minerals. The lowlands are primarily agricultural. Textiles, chemicals, and processed foods are major industries in the South. Southern products are easily distributed outside the area because of the fine ports and harbors along the coast.

The South was the scene of the Civil War. The conflict between the North and South began in 1861 and ended on April 9, 1865. Reconstruction followed the war and was over by 1877. Because plantation owners had no slaves after the war, they rented their land to tenant farmers for a share of the crop. Much of the land was depleted through the farming methods of the sharecroppers.

The Midwest. The states in the Midwest include Illinois, Indiana, Iowa, Kansas, Michigan, Minnesota, Missouri, Nebraska, North Dakota, Ohio, Oklahoma, South Dakota, Texas, and Wisconsin.

The landform of the western half of the Midwest is a vast plains area called the Great Plains. Two highland areas are in the plains: the South Dakota Black Hills and the Badlands. The Great Plains lie in the rain shadow of the Rocky Mountains and receive little rain. Some farmers use irrigation to grow crops; others use the land for grazing.

The landforms of the eastern half of the Midwest include the Central Lowlands, the Superior Upland, and other highland areas. The Superior Upland is characterized by dense forests, hills, and thousands of lakes. This part of the region has many summer thunderstorms.

The Midwest has a continental climate: very cold winters and very warm summers. One of the most valuable resources of this region is fertile soil. The growing season is about three

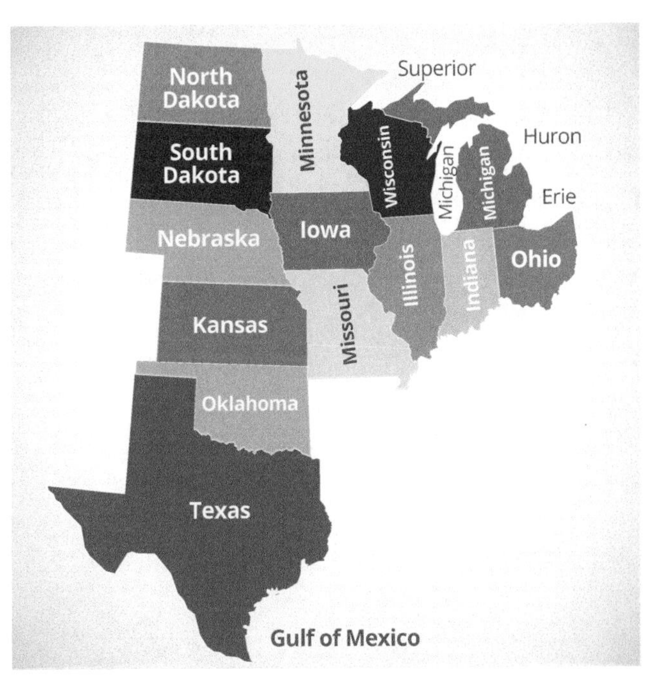

| Midwestern States

months long in the northern part of this region and is about nine months long in the southern part. The three most important agricultural areas are the "corn belt," the "wheat belt," and the "hay and dairy belt." The products from these areas supply much of the nation's food. However, weather disasters such as floods, hail, and tornadoes threaten and destroy some of these crops every year.

Thousands of pioneers followed Daniel Boone through the Cumberland Gap in 1775 to settle the Midwest. Many native Americans living in this area were forced to relocate in Oklahoma, the Indian Territory. The Five Civilized Tribes—Creek, Cherokee, Choctaw, Chickasaw, and Seminole—were moved from their territory in the South to Oklahoma.

Modern industry in the Midwest includes steel mills and manufacturing in the north. Meat packing and food processing plants are also found in the north. The southern section has many oil fields and refineries.

The West. Spanish explorers led by Coronado came to this region in 1540. Settlers came many years later. Santa Fe, the oldest capital city in the nation, was founded in 1609. San Francisco and San Diego were not settled until 1769. Los Angeles, the largest city in the region, was not established until 1781.

The states in the West are Alaska, Arizona, California, Colorado, Hawaii, Idaho, Montana, Nevada, New Mexico Oregon, Utah, Washington, and Wyoming.

The landforms include the highest point in the United States, Denali, Alaska, and the lowest point, Death Valley, California. The geography of the West includes the Great Plains, the Rocky Mountains, the Intermountain region, the Pacific Coast Mountain and Valley region, the landforms of the Alaskan peninsula and islands and the Volcanic Rock region of the Hawaiian Islands.

Many plateaus exist in the Intermountain region. One plateau, the Colorado Plateau, is the site of the Grand Canyon. This canyon is located in Arizona and channels the Colorado River.

The Intermountain region also contains several basins. Because basins have no drainage to the sea, water collects in ponds and lakes. The water then evaporates leaving salt deposits. The Great Salt Lake in Utah is located in the Great Basin.

The climate of the West varies greatly. The southern Intermountain region is desert,

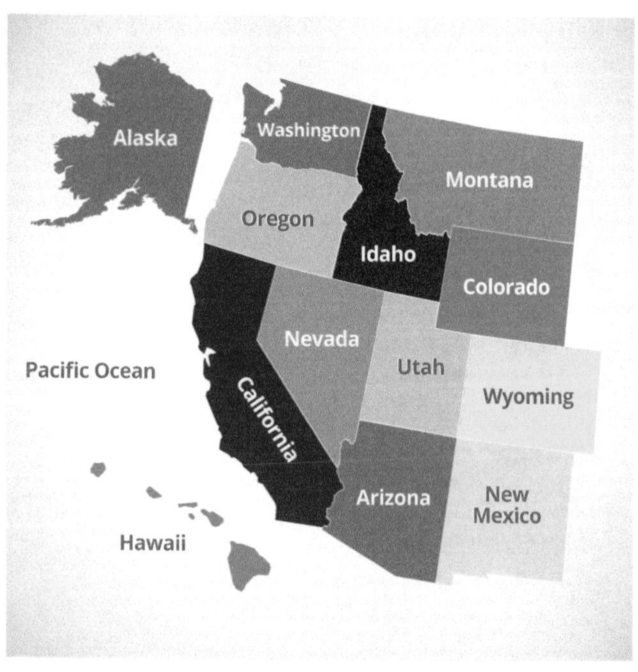

| Western States

having very little rainfall. The temperature in the southern part of this region is sometimes above 120 degrees. Parts of Hawaii and Washington receive more than two hundred inches of rain each year. The temperature in Alaska is often 30 degrees below zero.

The West produces timber for wood pulp and many food crops. Mining and fishing also contribute greatly to the economy of the West. Metal fabrication, oil refineries, and food processing plants are major industries in this region.

Write *true* or *false*.

1.72 ____________ Before European explorers arrived, no people were living in North America.

1.73 ____________ All fifty states of the United States are contiguous and lie on the North American continent.

1.74 ____________ Europeans began exploring parts of North America more than 900 years ago.

1.75 ____________ The earliest explorers were searching for wealth, not for a new home.

1.76 ____________ The early history of the United States was affected by landforms, climate, and natural resources.

Complete these statements.

1.77 The a. ______________________ United States was the scene of two revolutions: the Revolutionary War and the b. ______________________ Revolution.

1.78 Midwestern climate is characterized by very a. ________________ winters and b. ________________ summers.

1.79 The Five Civilized Tribes were the a. ______________________,
b. ______________________, c. ______________________,
d. ______________________, and e. ______________________.

1.80 The South and the West were first explored by the ______________________.

Complete these activities.

1.81 Put a letter beside each landform or state indicating which region it is in—*N* for Northeast; *S* for South; *M* for Midwest; *W* for West.

a. _____ Great Plains
b. _____ Oklahoma
c. _____ Denali
d. _____ Oregon
e. _____ Georgia
f. _____ Ozark Highlands

1.82 Put a letter beside each land form of state indicating which region it is in—*N* for Northeast; *S* for South; *M* for Midwest; *W* for West.

a. _____ Piedmont Plateau
b. _____ Rocky Mountains
c. _____ Northern Appalachian Highlands
d. _____ Death Valley
e. _____ Superior Uplands
f. _____ Maine

Review the material in this section in preparation for the Self Test. The Self Test will check your mastery of this particular section. The items missed on this Self Test will indicate specific areas where restudy is needed for mastery.

SELF TEST 1

Match these terms (each answer, 2 points).

1.01 _______ Mariana Trench
1.02 _______ primary source
1.03 _______ secondary source
1.04 _______ longitude
1.05 _______ delta
1.06 _______ climatology
1.07 _______ equinox
1.08 _______ interrupted-area projection
1.09 _______ archaeological remains
1.010 _______ equator
1.011 _______ latitude
1.012 _______ polar projection

a. study of average weather
b. used in mapping airplane routes
c. lowest point of earth's surface
d. lines extending east and west
e. information from the same period as the one being studied
f. imaginary circle around the middle of the earth
g. information from a period later than the one being studied
h. may contain pottery, tools, bones
i. lines extending from the North Pole to the South Pole
j. has blank spaces
k. triangular piece of land at the mouth of a river
l. nights are twelve hours long

Write the letter for the correct answer on each line (each answer, 2 points).

1.013 Geographical features such as mountains, plains, and oceans are _______ .
a. contiguous b. projections c. reliefs d. meridians

1.014 The Greek sense of history was _______ .
a. linear b. spherical c. cyclical d. physical

1.015 In how many different time zones do the continental United States lie? _______
a. twenty-four b. twelve c. seven d. four

1.016 The shape of the earth is _______ .
a. a perfect sphere b. an imperfect sphere
c. a large cone d. flat

1.017 The Bible provides the total picture of history from _______ .
a. Creation to the Fall b. King David to Jesus Christ
c. the Fall to salvation d. Creation to eternity

Complete these statements (each answer, 3 points).

1.018 The definition of history used in this unit is: "History is the known story of man and his relationship to a. ___________, to b. ___________, and to his c. ________________________."

1.019 The study of the features of the earth is ________________________ geography.

1.020 The a. ________________________ were the first Europeans to explore the b. ________________________ region and establish its first settlement, St. Augustine, Florida.

1.021 Approximately ____________________ percent of the earth's surface is covered by water.

1.022 History began with ______________, before Creation.

Write *true* or *false* (each answer, 1 point).

1.023 __________ Books, diaries, and manuscripts are written records that are valuable to historians.

1.024 __________ Early settlers' lives were not affected by regional landforms.

1.025 __________ Dates assigned to the earth and to its prehistoric remains are only estimates.

1.026 __________ Historical data may include both archaeological remains and written records.

1.027 __________ The periods of light and darkness over most of the earth are produced by the movement of the earth.

1.028 __________ Each of the world's twenty-four time zones represents one hour of time.

1.029 __________ The 180th meridian is the International Date Line.

1.030 __________ The West was the scene of the Civil War.

1.031 __________ The cities of the fall line were established where the Mississippi River comes out of the Rocky Mountains.

Complete these activities (each answer, 3 points).

1.032 Ancient civilizations that made valuable contributions to history include the:

a. ______________________ b. ______________________ ,

c. ______________________ d. ______________________ .

1.033 The highest point in the U.S., a. ________________ , and the lowest point,

b. ______________ Valley, are in the c. ______________ region.

1.034 Two revolutions occurred in the Northeast: the a. ________________ War and the

b. ________________ Revolution.

Write ***true*** **or** ***false*** (each answer, 1 point).

1.035 __________ Early Spanish explorers in the South and West were seeking wealth rather than new homes.

1.036 __________ The North American Plains is one of the three major plains areas in the world.

1.037 __________ The Mercator projection, using lines of latitude, is helpful in determining directions.

1.038 __________ Archives usually contain primary sources for the historian, and libraries usually contain secondary sources.

1.039 __________ The essential nature of man has remained the same from the Fall to the present time.

1.040 __________ Man is engaged in spiritual, human, and natural areas of conflict.

80/100 **SCORE** __________ **TEACHER** __________ __________
initials date

2. ANTHROPOLOGY AND SOCIOLOGY

Anthropology and sociology are two related areas of study concerned with groups of people and their institutions. Both the anthropologist and the sociologist are interested in man's culture. Although no two societies are identical, all human groups have many elements in common. Anthropologists use the comparative method to discover similarities and differences among societies. Fieldwork provides much of the data for the study of man's way of life. The sociologist is concerned with the study of the groups that made up society. Philosophers long ago thought about an ideal society, called **utopia**, but the science of sociology is relatively new.

In this section of the LIFEPAC you will learn about the **disciplines** of anthropology and sociology. You will learn the methods social scientists use to study man and society. You will also learn that the culture of any group of people is directly influenced by its environment.

Most citizens of the United States are not "Native Americans." Rather, they are immigrants or descendants of immigrants. You will learn that the United States, once called "a melting pot" of cultures, is today becoming more of a **pluralistic** society. You will learn some of the elements involved in cultural change and continuity.

SECTION OBJECTIVES

Review these objectives. When you have completed this section, you should be able to:

5. Describe the tools and methods of the anthropologist and sociologist.
6. Explain the origin and nature of culture and of social institutions.
7. Tell how culture is influenced by environment.
8. List elements of social change.

VOCABULARY

Study these words to enhance your learning success in this section.

acculturation (u kul' chu rā' shun). Borrowing between societies resulting in new cultural patterns.

allele (u lēl'). One of a gene pair.

artifact (är' tu fakt). Object made by human skills.

assimilation (u sim' u lā' shun). Process of becoming alike or similar.

bias (bī us). Favoring one side over the other.

bipedal (bī' pu dul). Having two feet.

confound (kon found'). Confuse.

determinism (di tėr' mun iz um). Belief that all events are the result of other events that have occurred before.

dialect (dī' u lekt). Speech sounds or patterns of a particular region.

discipline (dis' u plin). A field of study.

emigrate (em' u grāt). Leave one's own country to settle in another.

function (fungk' shun). Purpose for which something is used or intended.

genealogical (jē nē u loj' u kul). Concerning family descent.

genus (jē' nus). A group of similar things.

heterozygous (het' ur u zī gus). Having different alleles for one gene.

homozygous (hō mu zī' gus). Having identical alleles for one gene.

horticulturists (hôr' tu kul' chur ists). People who grow food crops.

hypothesis (hī poth' u sis). Something assumed to be true.

immigrants (im' u grunts). Persons who come into a foreign country to live.

magic (maj' ik). Use of secret charms and spells to make things happen.

monograph (mon' u graf). A scholarly book about one particular subject.

nomad (nō' mad). Member of a tribe that moves from place to place.

nonliterate (non lit' ur it). A term used in Anthropology to refer to a people or culture without a written language; also referred to as an oral society.

oracle (ôr' u kul). Means of obtaining a yes or no answer to some question.

palisade (pal' u sād'). Fence of wooden stakes used for defense.

pastoralists (pas' tur ul ists). People who depend on animal herds for food.

pluralism (plu̇r' u liz' um). Society in which several different racial or religious groups fully participate.

positivism (poz' u tiv iz' um). Philosophy that accepts only knowledge based on facts.

pueblo (pweb' lō). An Indian village in the Southwest.

race (rās). A group of people who share the same ancestry and physical traits.

sachem (sā' chum). Iroquois tribal leader.

stereotype (ster' ē u tīp). An oversimplified mental picture held by members of a group.

utopia (yu̇ to' pē u). An imaginary perfect place or society.

valid (val' ud). Supported by facts.

THE STUDY OF MAN

Many areas of study are concerned with man. Psychology is concerned with the individual and his adjustment to society. Economics is the study of the goods and services a society produces. History is concerned with the past events that have affected groups of people. Political science is the study of the principles and conduct of government. Philosophy is the study of knowledge and deals with the problem of epistemology, how we know what we know. Two related disciplines, or areas of study, are concerned with groups of people and their institutions: anthropology and sociology.

The discipline of anthropology. The word *anthropology* means *the study of man.* The

| Understanding Culture from the Inside

science of anthropology is divided into three special studies: archaeology, ethnology, and physical anthropology. Archaeology is concerned with man's way of life in the past. Ethnology is concerned with man's way of life in the present. Physical anthropology is concerned with the physical characteristics of people as evidenced in ancient bones and modern races.

The central problem of anthropology is culture. Culture is any information or behavior that is learned, shared by society, and passed on to the next generation. When God made man, He told him (Genesis 1:28) to "...be fruitful, and multiply, and replenish the earth, and subdue it..." Culture is how man subdues his environment.

The goal of anthropology is to discover the regularities of culture. Although no two cultures are identical, all social groups have many elements in common. Anthropologists want to explain why people who are so scattered from each other do the same kinds of things. They also want to explain the differences among groups of people. For instance, all groups have names to refer to relatives. Anthropologists want to explain why a father's brother is called an "uncle" in some groups and a "father" in other groups.

Anthropologists use the comparative method to discover similarities and differences among societies. By comparing many societies, anthropologists have developed a world-wide background that helps them to understand something about a single society.

The science of anthropology is grounded in fieldwork, studying people as they live. Fieldwork requires much preparation. The ethnographer is expected to be in the field at least one year to see all the seasonal activities. He must be prepared physically, emotionally, and spiritually for the culture shock that comes with adjusting to a new way of life.

In the field the ethnographer is a participant-observer. He learns about a society's culture by living according to that society's standards; he writes down what he observes. He also gathers special information from key informants.

To understand the behavior between persons, the ethnographer must know their relationship. He discovers kinship relationships by using the **genealogical** method, asking how relatives are addressed in that society.

Psychological tests, life histories, censuses, and maps are useful tools to the ethnographer. However, the most useful tool is the language of the group under study. The language reveals how the group relates to the world.

The findings of the ethnographer must not be **biased**. He must avoid both ethnocentrism and the "noble savage" bias. Ethnocentrism is concluding that a foreign culture is inferior to one's own culture. The "noble savage" bias is concluding that a foreign **nonliterate** culture is superior to one's own.

After his field notes are analyzed, the ethnographer will present his findings. The findings of fieldwork are often presented in either a general **monograph**, a specialized monograph, or a life-history account. Recently, however, ethnographic films have become widely used. Films show movement, space, shape, and tempo—important aspects of a culture. Films also provide a historical record that allows a cultural event of the past to be compared with the same event of the present. This comparison is useful for studying cultural changes.

Match these vocabulary terms with their definitions.

2.1 ________ acculturation
2.2 ________ allele
2.3 ________ assimilation
2.4 ________ bias
2.5 ________ bipedal
2.6 ________ confound
2.7 ________ determinism
2.8 ________ discipline
2.9 ________ positivism

a. borrowing between societies resulting in new cultural patterns
b. philosophy that accepts only knowledge based on facts
c. one of a gene pair
d. a field of study
e. process of becoming alike or similar
f. belief that all events are the result of other events that have occurred before
g. favoring one side over the other
h. to confuse
i. having two feet

Complete these statements.

2.10 Archaeology is concerned with man's way of life in the ________________________ .

2.11 Ethnology is concerned with man's way of life in the ________________________ .

2.12 Physical ________________________________ is concerned with man's physical characteristics.

2.13 ________________________ is how man subdues his environment.

2.14 The most useful tool to the ethnographer is the ________________________________ of the group he is studying.

 **Write *true* or *false*.**

2.15 ____________ Cultures everywhere are identical.

2.16 ____________ Anthropologists use the comparative method to help them understand societies.

2.17 ____________ Fieldwork requires the anthropologist to live for at least a year among the people being studied.

2.18 ____________ Motion picture films have no place in the ethnographer's work.

2.19 ____________ A monograph is a scholarly book about one particular subject.

2.20 ____________ The "noble savage" bias means the ethnographer believes that a foreign, nonliterate culture is inferior to his own.

2.21 ____________ The ethnographer attempts to discover kinship by asking how relatives are addressed in a particular society.

2.22 ____________ Ethnocentrism is concluding that a foreign culture is inferior to one's own culture.

2.23 ____________ Family relationships are not important in understanding the behavior between persons.

2.24 ____________ The language of the group being studied reveals how the group relates to the world.

Complete the crossword.

2.25 ACROSS

1. Having different alleles for one gene.
2. A scholarly book about one particular subject.
3. Concerning family descent.
4. An imaginary perfect place or society.
5. Persons who come into a foreign country to live.
6. Not able to read or to write.

DOWN

1. Having identical alleles for one gene.
2. A group of people who share the same ancestry and physical traits.
3. A group of similar things.
4. Supported by facts.
5. Purpose for which something is used or intended.
6. Something assumed to be true.

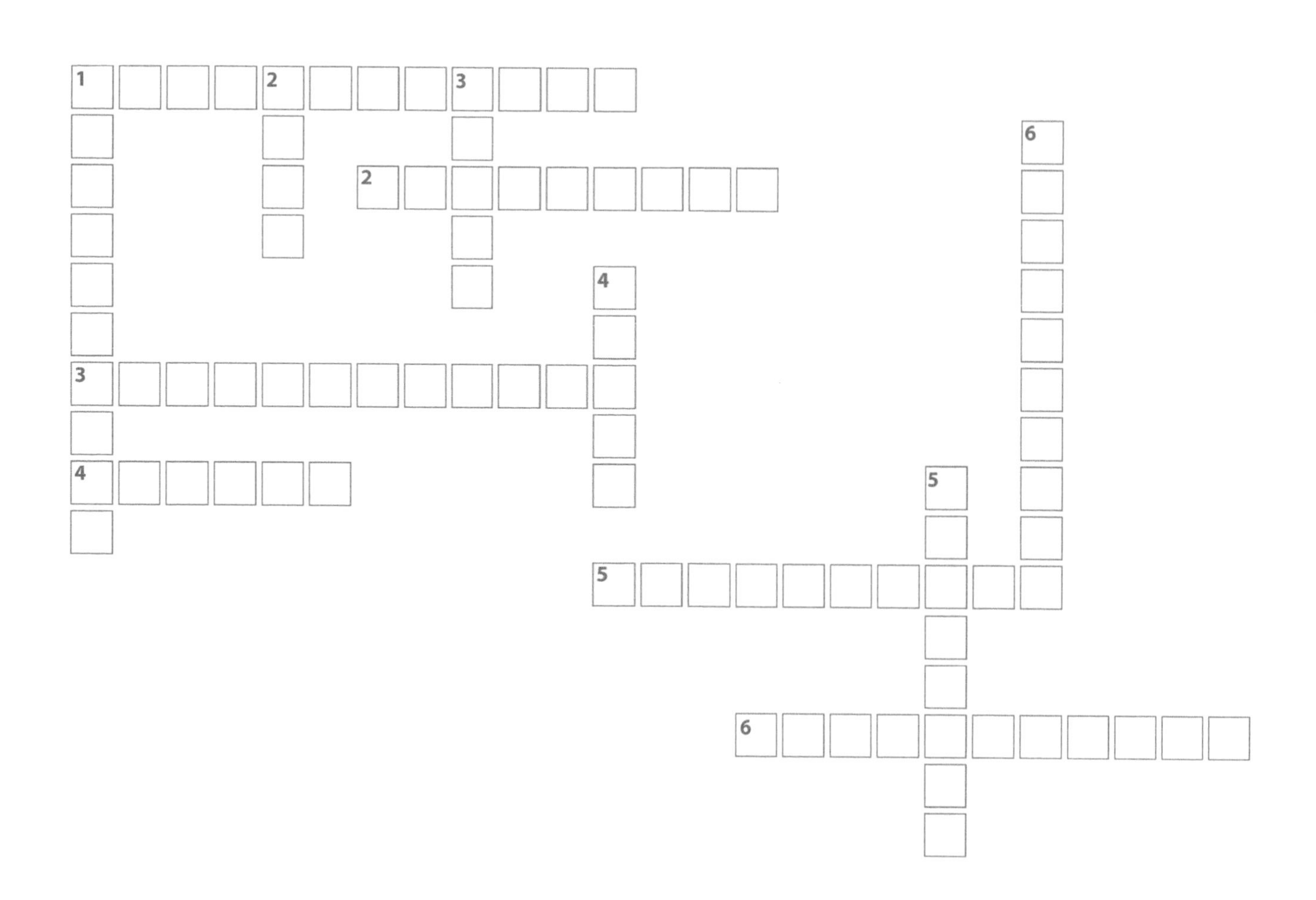

The discipline of sociology. The science of sociology is concerned with the study of social groups. As a science, sociology is quite recent. However, men have thought about society throughout history. Plato, Aristotle, Thomas More, Francis Bacon, Jonathan Swift saw the problems of their societies and made comments on their solutions. For instance, Plato imagined an idealistic society where philosopher-kings would rule the two classes of the workers and the soldiers. Any such ideal type of society is called a **utopia**.

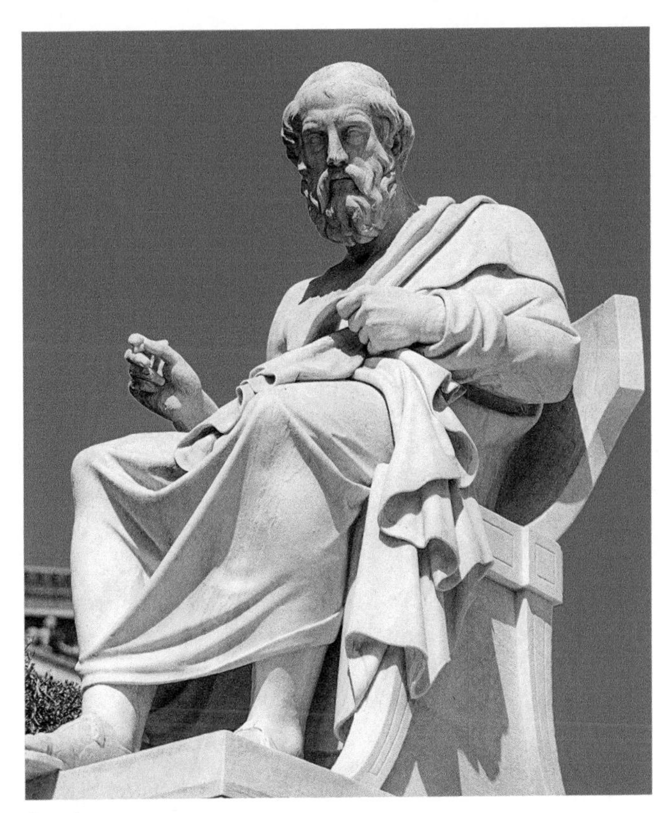

| Plato

More recent sociological thinkers include Auguste Comte, Karl Marx, Herbert Spencer, Emile Durkheim, and Max Weber. Auguste Comte first used the word *sociology* and is considered the "Father of Sociology." He discounted knowledge gained through faith and reason. Only the knowledge based on the observation of facts (**positivism**) was correct according to Comte.

Karl Marx said that all social institutions and changes are controlled by economic forces. His theory is called "economic **determinism**" and is described in his book *Das Kapital*.

| Auguste Comte

Herbert Spencer tried to apply the theory of biological evolution to society. Society was viewed as evolving from lower to higher forms. Emile Durkheim was the first to use scientific methods of data collection and observation in his sociological work. Max Weber thought of social structure and social action as ideal types. His work, *The Protestant Ethic and the Spirit of Capitalism*, said that the free enterprise system was closely related to the rise of Protestantism.

The Scriptures present much information on two institutions of interest to sociologists, the family and the churc`h. The Bible also records the history of an ancient society, the Jews, and presents many of society's problems and their solutions. The Lord Jesus Christ alone can remedy the sin-caused problems of society.

Sociologists study the groups that make up society. Groups can be distinguished by their

functions. A group that serves a particular purpose for a limited period of time is called an association. A group that serves a public purpose for a long period of time is called an institution.

Groups can also be distinguished according to the amount of personal involvement required. Primary groups are characterized by total involvement. Secondary groups are characterized by only partial involvement.

The family is the best example of a primary group. Members of a family are committed to each other for love, support and help in time of need. Two basic types of families exist: the nuclear family and the extended family. The nuclear family includes the father, the mother, and the children. The extended family includes a person's cousins, aunts, uncles, and grandparents.

Secondary groups are large and may contain several primary groups. A secondary group is more formal than a primary group. Examples of a secondary group include clubs, factories, and communities.

Culture refers to the knowledge and skills used within a society. Sociologists and anthropologists are interested in culture. They have discovered that culture is transmitted primarily through language.

| Karl Marx

Culture can be changed in several ways. **Acculturation** is the process of change in cultures when two large societies interact. Cultural **assimilation** occurs when one culture is assimilated into another, more dominant culture. Cultural diffusion is the spread of a cultural trait from one society to another. Because cultural elements are so easily shared today, the world's cultures are rapidly changing. Some sociologists believe that the world may be moving toward a single culture.

| Nuclear Family

| Extended Family

Write *true* or *false*.

2.26 ____________ As a science, sociology is as old as history.

2.27 ____________ Utopia is an idealized society.

2.28 ____________ Positivists accept only the knowledge based on observed facts.

2.29 ____________ Sociologists study the groups and institutions that make up society.

Match the following. Two items may apply.

2.30 _______ Plato

2.31 _______ Auguste Comte

2.32 _______ Karl Marx

2.33 _______ Herbert Spencer

2.34 _______ Emile Durkheim

2.35 _______ Max Weber

a. coined the word *sociology*

b. applied theory of biological evolution to society

c. used scientific methods of data collection

d. *The Protestant Ethic* and the *Spirit of Capitalism*

e. imagined an idealized society

f. father of sociology

g. thought of social structure and social action as ideal types

h. *Das Kapital*

Complete these statements.

2.36 The Scriptures present information on two important social institutions, the a. ____________________ and the b. ____________________ .

2.37 A group that serves a particular purpose for a limited period of time, such as a club, is called a(n) ____________________ .

2.38 A group that serves a public purpose for a longer period of time, such as the family, is called a(n) ____________________ .

2.39 Groups characterized by total involvement are called a. ____________________ groups, and groups characterized by only partial involvement are called b. ____________________ groups.

2.40 When two large societies interact by borrowing and trading, the process of ____________________ takes place.

2.41 When one culture is taken over or absorbed by a more dominant culture, the process of ____________________ takes place.

Socialization is the training a person receives so that he can function successfully in society. Socialization provides a person with these very important skills and attitudes:

1. Basic disciplines that allow a person to live an orderly life.
2. General life goals that give direction to life.
3. Basic social skills.
4. Knowledge of social roles.
5. Development of self-control.
6. Experience of being loved.
7. Development of a person's self-image.

Socialization is achieved through instruction, encouragement, and discipline. The best tool for socialization is the Bible. According to 2 Timothy 3:16 and 17, the Scriptures are "...profitable for doctrine, for reproof, for correction, for instruction in righteousness: That the man of God may be perfect, thoroughly furnished unto all good works."

People act differently in groups than they act as individuals. Relatively unorganized groups, such as people watching a basketball game, show a collective behavior. They usually act in unison and share the same emotional experience or mood. This characteristic is known as *emotional contagion*.

Public opinion is a form of collective behavior. People who share the same opinions often belong to the same groups. Public opinion is often influenced by propaganda, widespread appeals toward a certain position.

Sociologists are interested in the effects of certain things on a society. For instance, they study the effects of population, how people behave in overcrowded areas. They also study the effects of religion on society and the effects of one person's influence on a group. A Christian can influence a group for the Lord.

Sociologists use several methods in studying society. Classical theorists use logic and

| Collective Behavior

reasoning in their work and develop theories to explain what is supposed to happen in society. Besides theories, sociologists use description: words to tell how something actually happened. Description is objective reporting; theories are idealized concepts of all occurrences.

Another method used by sociologists is statistical analysis. This method tests **hypotheses** to determine how **valid** they are. Data that relates to some hypotheses are gathered and computed. After computation, the data shows the probability of the hypothesis being valid.

Sociological data usually are gathered by using a sociological survey. A survey is taken among a sample of a larger population. If a sample is selected from a representative group, the results of the survey will be accurate and valid for the whole population. A random sample is more general and less valid and accurate than a selected sample.

Sociologists sometimes use controlled experiments to see how a certain group will react in a certain situation. Groups used in an experiment are usually small. People in the groups are selected by age, sex, background, common interest, or any particular quality necessary for the experiment.

When a sociologist wants to learn how a particular group of people lives, he moves to that area. He may want to study life in a small farming town or in a large city. Living among the people being studied is called fieldwork.

 **Write *true* or *false*.**

2.42 ____________ The Holy Scriptures are the best tool for socialization.

2.43 ____________ People act exactly the same way in groups as they act as individuals.

2.44 ____________ Collective behavior means that people may act in unison and share the same emotional experience or mood.

2.45 ____________ Public opinion is never influenced by propaganda.

2.46 ____________ One Christian may influence the behavior and attitude of a group for the Lord.

2.47 ____________ Like the anthropologist, the sociologist may need to live among the people being studied.

Complete this sentence.

2.48 Socialization provides a person with a number of important skills and attitudes including

a. ______________________________, b. ______________________________,

c. ______________________________, and d. ______________________________.

THE NATURE OF MAN

When God made man, He created male and female. All people have come from this first couple; therefore, all people have much in common. Although the "cultural skin" people wear differs from group to group, the physical nature of man is everywhere the same. Physical differences do occur among **races**, but a person of one race is as much man as a person of another race.

The unity of man. People everywhere share the same ultimate origin, God, and the same physical ancestors, Adam and Eve. The body of every person is composed of the same materials commonly found in the earth and all human beings also have similar physical structures. We are **bipedal** and have paired extremities, opposable thumbs, eye/hand coordination, and a skeleton of 206 bones.

All people were made in the image of God. Being made in God's image means that man has great value and is like God in some ways. Like God, a person can know himself, be morally responsible, and extend grace to others.

| People have a common origin.

At one time all people had a common language. That language enabled them to work together. However, God was displeased with man's activity, and He **confounded** their language. Today, every society has its own meaningful language.

Adam has passed to all his descendants a heritage of sin and death. Jesus Christ has passed to those who believe on Him eternal life. These two heritages are presented in John 3:36:

"He that believeth on the Son hath everlasting life: and he that believeth not the Son shall not see life; but the wrath of God abideth on him."

Scientists have said all people belong to the **genus** *Homo* and to the species *sapiens*. The Bible says that all people have been made of one blood—they are the same kind. Being of one kind, any two people can reproduce and have fertile offspring who can also reproduce.

Complete these statements.

2.49 People everywhere share the same ancestors, known as a. ____________ and b. ____________ .

2.50 The body of every person is composed of materials commonly found in the ______________________ .

2.51 The human skeleton consists of ____________ bones.

2.52 At one time all people had a common ______________________ that enabled them to work together.

2.53 Jesus Christ gives to those who believe on Him ______________________ life.

2.54 Scientists have said that all people belong to the genus a. ______________________ and to the species b. ______________________ .

The diversity of man. No two people look exactly alike, and—except in the cases of identical twins, triplets, etc.—no two people have precisely the same genes. Genes are the material a person receives from his parents that determines his physical characteristics, or phenotype. Mother and father each contribute one **allele** for every gene in the child. When the two alleles for a gene are identical, the person is **homozygous** for that gene. When the two alleles are different, the person is **heterozygous** for that gene.

A group that is homozygous for many genes is a race. Man is usually divided into three races: Mongoloid, Negroid, and Europoid. These races are identified with the descendants of Noah: Shem, Ham, and Japheth. The noticeable areas of racial differences include physical height, facial features, skin color, and hair features.

Three elements are necessary to produce a race: a population, an environment, and a common language. A common language allows a population to develop a unique culture in a particular environment. Those who do not know the language of a people are prevented from living among them and from participating in their culture.

The people who were scattered from the city of Babel settled in separate parts of the earth. Because language was a barrier between people from different groups, marriages were made between people from the same group. Through generations of intermarriage, each of the groups from Noah's three sons became homozygous for many different genes. Their genetic distinctions have resulted in the three major races.

Complete these statements.

2.55 Three elements are necessary to produce a race: a. ______________________________,
b. ______________________________, and c. ______________________________.

2.56 Man is usually divided into three races: a. ______________________________,
b. ______________________________, and c. ______________________________.

2.57 Noticeable areas of racial differences include a. ______________________________,
b. ______________________________, c. ______________________________, and
d. ______________________________.

2.58 The three descendants of Noah from which the three races have resulted are
a. ____________________, b. ____________________, and c. ____________________.

Write *true* or *false*.

2.59 ______________ No two people have precisely the same genes.

2.60 ______________ A person's genes determine his physical characteristics, or phenotype.

2.61 ______________ People from the city of Babel settled in different parts of the earth.

2.62 ______________ Lack of common language serves as a barrier between people from different groups.

THE CULTURE OF MAN

Every human group has a culture—each group subdues its environment. The culture of a group reflects the characteristics of its environment. An environment contains certain kinds of plants and animals to be used as food. It also contains certain materials and other groups that can be used to provide protection. People in every society try to enhance their lives by controlling their environments through the use of some form of supernatural power.

Seeking food. People of small, nonliterate societies are labeled by anthropologists according to the way they obtain food. Hunters and gatherers usually wander in small groups looking for food. The size of the group depends on the amount of food available and the number of people required to obtain the food. The Arunta of Central Australia are a hunting and gathering people who subsist primarily on small animals and insects. They wander in bands of two or three families and must move after one or two days in an area. Their brush lean-to shelters are abandoned when they move.

Horticulturists rely on the natural fertility of the soil and on rain for a good crop. When the soil is depleted, usually in one or two years, they must relocate their fields. They stay close to their fields to protect them. Their shelters are more permanent than those of hunters and gatherers. The Yanomamö are South American horticulturists who live in large circular community houses. They relocate their communities when the soil in the village area is depleted or when friction between people is leading to warfare. The Hopi from northern Arizona are horticulturists whose soil is renewed by wind-blown top soil. They live in stone apartments on flat table-top mountains, and they do not have to relocate their villages.

Fishing communities usually do not have to be relocated. The food supply does not migrate and is not easily depleted. Fishing communities are characterized by durable houses, large food reserves, and wealth. The Haida of the Pacific shores of British Columbia are an example of a fishing society.

Pastoralists depend on herds of domesticated animals for their food. Because the herds are moved from one grazing land to another when the seasons change, pastoralists are **nomadic**. The Nuer of the southern Sudan in Africa are cattle pastoralists. The cattle provide everything the Nuer need for daily life.

 **Write *true* or *false*.**

2.63 ____________ Anthropologists label people of small, nonliterate societies according to the way they obtain their food.

2.64 ____________ The amount of food available determines the size of the group.

2.65 ____________ Horticulturists must have fertile soil and sufficient rain.

2.66 ____________ Some groups must relocate their fields and villages every few years.

2.67 ____________ Fishing villages must frequently move far inland.

2.68 ____________ Pastoralists must always live in one place to tend their flocks and herds.

HISTORY & GEOGRAPHY 710

LIFEPAC TEST

NAME ______________________

DATE ______________________

SCORE ______________________

HISTORY & GEOGRAPHY 710: LIFEPAC TEST

Match the following (each answer, 2 points).

1. _______ Hebrews
2. _______ equator
3. _______ archaeological remains
4. _______ primary source
5. _______ latitude
6. _______ longitude
7. _______ acculturation
8. _______ assimilation
9. _______ Adam and Eve
10. _______ utopia

a. contributed Old Testament literature
b. an idealized society
c. imaginary line around the center of the earth
d. the shared ancestors of all mankind
e. may contain pottery, tools, or bones
f. occurs when one culture is taken over by a more dominant culture
g. information from the same period as the one being studied
h. mutual change that occurs when two societies interact
i. imaginary lines extending east and west
j. imaginary line extending from north to south

Write the letter for the correct answer on each line (each answer, 2 points).

11. A political party is a _______ .
    a. celebration after the election
    b. group of voters who share a similar viewpoint
    c. ceremonial feast among Northwest Indians
    d. means of distributing wealth
12. The most important component of a culture is _______ .
    a. food, clothing, shelter
    b. a medium of exchange
    c. a common language
    d. some way to foretell the future
13. The Bible provides the total picture of history from _______ .
    a. Creation to the Fall
    b. King David to Jesus Christ
    c. the Fall to salvation
    d. Creation to the Judgment
14. The dates assigned to earth and to its prehistoric remains are _______ .
    a. forever constant
    b. always predictable
    c. only estimates
    d. accurate within a few years
15. Additions to the language, interaction of the people, or the development of new tools or machinery may result in _______ .
    a. cultural change
    b. cultural stability
    c. a shift to urban living
    d. a shift to rural living
16. Societies in which people depend on other people to supply their needs are _______ .
    a. primitive
    b. socialist
    c. communistic
    d. complex

Match these terms with their definitions (each answer, 2 points).

17. ________ reliefs
18. ________ culture
19. ________ sociology
20. ________ anthropology
21. ________ political science
22. ________ rationalism
23. ________ fideism
24. ________ economics
25. ________ physical geography
26. ________ hierarchy

a. way of knowing based on logical thinking
b. way of knowing based on an act of faith
c. the study of the rules and procedures man uses to govern himself
d. the study of the production, distribution, and consumption of wealth
e. the study of man's way of life
f. the study of the features of the earth
g. the study of man's social groups and institutions
h. government having higher and lower ranks
i. geographical features
j. the ways in which man subdues his environment

Write *true* or *false* (each answer, 1 point).

27. ____________ Most state legislatures are bicameral.
28. ____________ When the supply of a commodity exceeds the demand, prices generally rise.
29. ____________ The science of sociology is primarily concerned with the creation of an ideal society.
30. ____________ A shift from rural to urban living does much to relieve social tensions and hostilities.
31. ____________ A lobbyist represents a special interest before the judicial branch of the government.
32. ____________ The communistic economic system does not encourage private investment, competition, or profit.
33. ____________ The earth makes one complete rotation every twenty-four hours.
34. ____________ The life of the Nuer is an example of the adaptation of culture to environment.
35. ____________ Regional landforms had no effect on the culture of the Native Americans or the early settlers.

Match these items (each answer, 2 points).

36. ________ socialization
37. ________ landforms
38. ________ basic human needs
39. ________ executive branch
40. ________ racial physical characteristics
41. ________ economic systems
42. ________ ways of foretelling the future

a. magic, divination, oracles
b. basic discipline, life goals, development of self-control
c. free enterprise, socialism, communism
d. mountains, plains, seas, and oceans
e. skin color, hair texture
f. food, clothing, shelter
g. governor, lieutenant-governor, secretary of state

Complete these statements (each answer, 3 points).

43. Many immigrants came to the United States seeking a. ________________ freedom, b. ________________ freedom, an ________________ freedom.
44. The writings that give the total view of history, are the best tool for socialization, and provide guides for personal financial responsibility are the ________________ .
45. A form of prejudice that keeps us from seeing people as individuals who are valuable in God's eyes is ________________ .
46. ________________ is knowing based upon the physical senses.
47. Most people in the underdeveloped countries of the world support themselves by ________________ .
48. ________________ was the Greek philosopher who divided governments into those ruled by one, few, and many.
49. The sources of western political thought include a. ________________ , b. ________________ , and c. ________________ civilizations.

Complete the vocabulary crossword.

2.69 ACROSS
1. People who depend on animal herds for food.
2. Leave one's own country to settle in another.
3. Means of obtaining a yes or no answer to some question.
4. Object made by human skills.

DOWN
1. An Indian village in the Southwest.
2. Use of secret charms and spells to make things happen.
3. An oversimplified mental picture held by members of a group.

Match these vocabulary words with their definitions.

2.70 ______ dialect
2.71 ______ horticulturists
2.72 ______ nomad
2.73 ______ palisade
2.74 ______ pluralism
2.75 ______ sachem

a. member of a tribe that moves from place to place
b. people who grow food crops
c. fence of wooden stakes used for defense
d. society in which several different racial or religious groups participate fully
e. speech sounds or patterns of a particular region
f. Iroquois tribal leader

Seeking protection. People build shelters to provide protection from their environments. The size, style, and construction of a shelter will depend on the environment and on the culture of the society. For example, the Eskimos who hunt seal on the frozen Arctic Ocean build igloos out of hard snow, the most readily available material in that environment. Each igloo houses one family. Several igloos are clustered together because several men usually hunt together.

| Eskimo Igloo

People need to live near their food supplies. In general, those who depend on horticulture or fishing will have relatively permanent shelters. If one of these groups must shift its location, a new shelter will be built. The people who herd or hunt animals will use portable or disposable shelters.

Most small societies are groups of kin who stand together against their foes. An alliance can also be made between two unrelated groups for mutual support. Such an alliance is usually created by intermarriage. Intermarriage creates a tie of kinship between two groups, and kin have an obligation to help each other.

Complete these statements.

2.76 The a. ______________________ and the b. ______________________ of a society will determine the size, style, and construction of their shelters.

2.77 An alliance between two unrelated groups can be made by creating a kinship between them through ______________________ .

Seeking prosperity. People in every society depend on some form of supernatural power to give them success in life. The Crow Indians of the plains sought success, or power, through visions. A Crow might seek a vision by self-mutilation or fasting.

Many groups use **magic** to be successful. In anthropology *magic* is defined as *following a formula for doing things that are beyond one's personal power.* A Zande adding plant juice to his fields to grow a good crop is using magic. Drawing pictures of animals being wounded to produce a successful hunt is an instance of magic. To help a person recover by bandaging the arrow that wounded him is also depending on magic. However, only by depending on God's laws in creation will a person be successful in life.

Divination is any method of learning about the future or about things otherwise hidden. One form of divination is omens. Omens are almost always related to events of nature. They include relationships of the stars and planets and other celestial events. Animal behavior is also seen as an omen of warning or blessing in many societies.

Oracles are another form of divination. They require a manipulation or experiment to get a *yes* or a *no* answer. The Zande use several oracles, each to answer questions of differing importance. They use two sticks in a termite mound for answers to simple problems. For quick answers to everyday problems, a Zande will use a rubbing board. In matters of great importance, a Zande will use benge. This poison is fed to a chicken, and the decision based on the reaction of the chicken has the force of law.

| Zande Rubbing Board

Complete these activities.

2.78 List five ways that people depend upon to give them success in life.

a. ____________________

b. ____________________

c. ____________________

d. ____________________

e. ____________________

2.79 To an anthropologist, ____________________ is following a formula for doing things that are beyond one's personal power.

THE CULTURAL GROUPS OF THE UNITED STATES

Long before the Europeans entered North America, this land was populated by Native Americans. The cultures of the Native Americans varied from region to region. The style of shelter, food gathering techniques, clothing, and society were directly affected by the environment of each group.

When the United States government extended statehood to Alaska and to Hawaii, new cultures were added to the Union. Because the environments of the Eskimos and Hawaiians differed from those of the Native Americans, the cultures of these groups also differed. A culture is directly influenced by its environment.

Native Americans. Many archaeologists believe that the Native Americans came from Asia to North America across the Bering Strait. **Artifacts** from this period of early migration indicate that these people were hunters. As they spread across the North American continent, they developed several distinct cultures. Some groups continued to hunt and to gather, others began farming, and others developed fishing skills.

The earliest people to settle in the Northeast were fishermen and woodland hunters. Those who settled on the Atlantic Coastal Plain came to depend on agriculture. As agriculture developed, settlements enlarged, trade developed, and the cultures of the Northeast became more complex.

Two primary styles of shelter were used in this area: the one-family wigwam and the multi-family longhouse. The shelters were clustered inside a **palisade** close to the crops. The people grew corn, beans, squash, pumpkins, and tobacco. The crops were the responsibility of the women. The men provided meat for the diet by hunting.

The Iroquois tribes were widely known as great warriors. Their leaders were called **sachems** and were chosen by the women of the tribe. Five Iroquois tribes were united in an association called the League of the Great Peace. This political organization included elements of democracy and representative government.

When European fur traders came to the Northeast, the league controlled the trading rights in the area. The Iroquois also became friendly with the English and supported England against the colonies during the Revolutionary War. After the war many Native Americans were forced to **emigrate** west of the Mississippi River.

The tribes of the Southeast are known for the mounds built in that area. Some mounds are placed over gravesites; other mounds were used to elevate a temple or a chief's house. The largest temple mound, Monk's Mound, was built in Cahokia, Illinois.

The first Native Americans to settle in the Southeast found a plentiful food supply. In this area they experienced neither drought nor cold. These ideal conditions probably contributed greatly to the development of an extensive trading system.

Many of the Southeastern Native Americans lived in palisaded villages centered around flat-topped mounds. Their houses were rectangular with mud walls and thatched or cane roofs. In warmer regions unwalled houses with a raised platform and thatched roof were used.

Some tribes in the Southeast were familiar with class titles and class privileges. The Natchez were organized into four classes: the Great Sun, the Little Suns, the Honored Men, and the Stinkards. The Great Sun was the absolute ruler and was given great deference by his people.

The Five Civilized Tribes adopted much of the European culture in the Southeast. Many people from these groups even became Christians. One of the five tribes, the Cherokee, had its own written language. It was developed by Sequoyah after twelve years of research. Although the Cherokee published a newspaper, had a formal constitution, and wrote their own law code, their land was taken away and they were pushed into Oklahoma.

The Indians of the Great Plains became the **stereotype** of the Native American. They lived in tepees, hunted buffalo, wore fringed buckskin clothing and feather headdresses, rode ponies, and fought settlers. The first Native Americans

Wigwam

Longhouse

Tepee

on the plains were nomadic and followed the buffalo on foot. Before horses came into use in the eighteenth century, people used dogs to carry their burdens.

Two cultures emerged on the plains: semi-nomadic farmers and nomadic hunters. The groups that depended on the buffalo wasted nothing of the animal. The flesh was eaten. The skin was used for clothing, blankets, and tepees; and the bones and horns were made into tools and utensils. Sign language was used for cross-cultural communication.

The Native Americans fought to preserve their land and their culture. However, the land was taken by incoming settlers, and the buffalo were killed for fun and profit by white hunters. Most plains tribes were confined to reservations by 1887.

An early culture of the Southwest was the Anasazi. These people lived in towering **pueblos** built on a canyon floor or in a recess on the face of the cliff. They had a farming economy with some hunting and gathering.

The pueblo people were skillful craftsmen. They made baskets, pottery jewelry, and cloth. Archaeologists believe the large pueblos were abandoned because of drought or incoming people with different values. Smaller pueblo groups, such as the Hopi and the Zuni, were encountered by the Spanish in the 1520s and still thrive today.

Many tribes lived in the Great Basin, a dry area with few large animals. Some tribes used pointed sticks to dig up insects, roots, and other food from the ground. They were called Digger Indians.

The Utes in the Great Basin had horses and raided ranches and pueblos for food, livestock, and slaves. They sold the slaves in the Spanish market in New Mexico.

California had more than one hundred five distinct tribes and branches of tribes. The abundant acorn crop allowed a large population

| Pueblos

and rich ceremonial life to develop. The staple acorn was supplemented with fish, wild plants, and small animals. California Native Americans are known for fine basketry.

Many Native Americans were forced to live close to the Spanish missions along the California coast. These groups forgot their old culture and did not survive when the missions closed.

The Native Americans of the Northwest Coast had an abundant food supply of fish, sea animals, and plant food from the forests. They developed a complex society and an elaborate culture. Their society was divided into three social classes: the chiefs, the freedmen, and the slaves.

The Northwest Coast people were noted woodworkers. They made dugout canoes that carried forty men. Their dwellings were made of cedar planks and housed several families each. With their stone and bone tools they carved masks, helmets, armor, boxes, utensils, and totem poles.

The great wealth in this area was periodically redistributed in a potlatch celebration. The chief who held the potlatch gained great status by giving away his own wealth and the wealth of his village. The recipients of the potlatch were obligated to return a greater amount of goods in a future potlatch.

Complete these statements.

2.80 Long before Europeans arrived, North America was populated by

________________________ .

2.81 The environment of each group of Native Americans directly affected their

a. ________________________ , b. ________________________ ,

c. ________________________ , and d. ________________________ .

2.82 The United States became a ________________________ pot for many different cultures.

2.83 Native Americans may have originally come across the

a. ________________________ from b. ________________________ .

2.84 Artifacts found from the early migrations indicate that these people probably made their living as ________________________ .

2.85 As the natives spread across the North American continent, they developed different and distinct ________________________ .

2.86 Sequoyah spent twelve years researching and developing a ________________________ language for the Cherokee.

2.87 Iroquois tribal leaders were chosen by the women of the tribe and were called

________________________ .

Match these items. Two or more items may apply.

2.88 ________ Northwest Coast tribes

2.89 ________ Southwest tribes

2.90 ________ Great Plains tribes

2.91 ________ Northeast tribes

2.92 ________ Southeast tribes

2.93 ________ Five Civilized Tribes

2.94 ________ Great Basin tribes

a. protected their homes with palisades

b. known as mound builders

c. used pointed sticks to dig for food

d. became Christians

e. encountered by the Spanish in 1520s

f. had an abundant supply of seafood

g. became stereotype of North American Indian

h. lived in tepees, hunted buffalo

i. carved totem poles; wood craftsmen

j. lived in pueblos or cliff dwellings

k. published their own newspaper

l. held ceremonial potlatches

Eskimos and Hawaiians. Eskimos are different from any Native American group in language, body type, and culture. Two major groups of Eskimos exist: Arctic Ocean Eskimos and Pacific Coast Eskimos.

Eskimo is a word that means *eaters of raw meat*. Eskimos fished or hunted for food. The coastal people depended primarily on the seal, and the inland people depended primarily on the caribou. The skins of the animals were used for clothing and summer tents. Winter houses were built by digging a pit and erecting a frame of wood or whalebone over it. The frame was covered with blocks of sod, and the inside was lined with bark or woven grass mats. Shelters called igloos could also be built from blocks of snow during the winter.

The Eskimo were the first people on the North American continent to make a lamp. They used a stone bowl, animal fat for fuel, and moss for a wick. They also made skin boats and wooden sleds for transportation.

Eskimo families sometimes lived by themselves. However, a few families would often cluster together to increase their success in a hunt.

The Hawaiian Islands were peopled by **immigrants** coming from the Marquesas Islands and from Tahiti. These people brought with them various plants and animals to be raised on the islands.

Men did the fishing, gardening, and cooking for the family. Food was cooked in a pit covered with dirt. Fish were an important part of the diet.

Women made sails, mats, and clothing. Clothes were made from decorated tapa cloth. Women also had housing separate from the men.

Each island had one king and many chiefs. The king was very important and received a share of the people's food supply. Chiefs would sometimes fight over land or other resources.

Complete these statements.

2.95 The word *Eskimo* means a. ________________ of b. ________________ meat.

2.96 The Eskimo people were the first on the North American continent to make a ____________________ .

2.97 The original inhabitants of Hawaii emigrated from a. ________________ and the b. ______________________________ Islands.

Complete this activity.

2.98 Give examples of the interrelation between the Eskimo's culture and his environment.

____

____

____

____

____

____

Immigrants. Most of the United States citizens are not "Native Americans"; they are descendants of immigrants who entered the country in the last four hundred years. The most dominant culture in the **pluralistic** society of the United States is that of the Anglo-Saxon Protestants. This cultural group has come primarily from Great Britain.

Many of the immigrants came to the United States to escape religious and political persecution. Some came to escape economic deprivation. For instance, between 1840 and 1860 the largest group of immigrants was from Ireland. They were escaping a serious potato famine.

The largest national group to come to the United States since 1820 has been the Germans. Many of them settled in Lancaster, Pennsylvania and are known as the "Pennsylvania Dutch." The second largest group is the Italians.

Immigrants from many western European nations have settled in the United States. Large communities of French settled in the southern Louisiana territory. The Dutch established communities of dairymen in the West, and many raise tulips or manufacture furniture in the Midwest. Scandinavians also settled in the Midwest on dairy and wheat farms. Many Greeks came even when economic conditions were poor in the United States.

In the late 1890s a wave of immigrants came from central Europe. Many Czechoslovakians settled in cities in the Northeast and on farms in the Great Lakes area. Many Polish people settled in mining villages and mill towns. Many Russians found jobs in the fur trade of Alaska and the Northwest.

The Japanese did not emigrate to the United States until 1885. Many Japanese worked as farmers along the Pacific coast. During World War II the Japanese were confined in relocation camps in several states. Many Japanese live in Hawaii.

The Chinese who came to the West Coast came looking for gold. Many found work on the railroads and as servants. The community of Chinese in San Francisco is larger than any other outside of Asia.

Most of the African people who came to the United States came as slaves. Almost all the ties to African culture were broken though their servitude. The Africans were quickly assimilated into the dominant culture of the eastern and southern United States.

People can be grouped in many ways. One way is according to ethnicity. An ethnic group is a group whose members share a culture that is different from other groups in the society. The Hispanic, or Spanish-speaking, people are an ethnic group.

The largest Hispanic group in the United States is Mexican. Most people of Mexican descent live in the Southwest and have strong cultural ties with Mexico. Los Angeles, California, is surpassed only by Mexico City, Mexico, in size of its Mexican population.

Many groups from both eastern and southern Europe did not wish to lose their ethnic identity in the United States. Consequently, they formed ethnic neighborhoods and communities. Cultural pluralism was expanding. New immigration laws favored those from northern and western Europe, those who would blend in with the dominant culture.

Ethnic groups often become stereotyped by the larger society. Stereotyping is a form of prejudice that keeps us from seeing people as individuals who are valuable in God's sight. Stereotyping also encourages people to discriminate against others.

Besides ethnicity, people can be grouped according to religion, region, social class, and occupation. Many people who immigrated to the United States did so for freedom of worship. The Jews have long been persecuted as a religious group. Many Jewish immigrants helped to build the United States, and they now number over 7 million in this country. Roman Catholics also fled persecution in the countries where they lived. About 50 million Catholics now live in the United States.

Regional groups share many values. They also often share a **dialect**.

Members of a social class share values, beliefs, and behaviors. One's social class affects the way he sees himself and others. It also influences the way people react to each other. The class structure of a society is usually determined by three factors: amount of money, type of work, and amount of education.

Social class should not become a reason to think one person is more important than another. In Romans 12:3 the Bible teaches a person "...not to think of himself more highly than he ought to think...."

Complete these sentences.

2.99 Many immigrants came to the United States to escape a. ______________________________ ,

b. ______________________________ , and

c. ______________________________ .

2.100 Stereotyping is a form of ____________________ that keeps us from seeing people who are valuable in God's sight.

2.101 Stereotyping may lead to ____________________ against others.

Match the following.

2.102 ______ Great Britain

2.103 ______ Ireland

2.104 ______ German

2.105 ______ French

2.106 ______ Africans

2.107 ______ Hispanic people

2.108 ______ Chinese

2.109 ______ Japanese

a. southern Louisiana

b. southwestern states

c. relocated during World War II

d. found work in the gold fields and on the railroads

e. potato famine

f. largest immigrant group since 1820

g. Anglo-Saxon Protestants

h. came as slaves

Complete this activity.

2.110 Tell what Indian tribes, immigrant groups, or religious sects and denominations are closely identified with the history and settlement of your region of the United States.

____

____

____

____

TEACHER CHECK __________ initials __________ date

SOCIAL CHANGE IN THE UNITED STATES

The United States is a melting pot of values, customs, behaviors, and beliefs. The culture of this country is widely shared among its inhabitants. Anthropologists and sociologists agree that a shared culture helps to hold a society together. They also agree that cultures change, and sudden changes can cause tensions in a society. The United States has experienced both cultural and structural changes. However, as changes occur, more interaction takes place among the people, and the culture becomes richer and more varied.

Cultural change. Language is a most important component of culture. Most citizens of the United States speak the same language—English. Everyone uses body language, facial expressions, and gestures. However, the spoken word is the primary vehicle for cultural continuity and change.

The early immigrants in the United States learned new words to name the new things they saw. These new words were primarily Native American words. The spelling and sounds of some words were changed before they were adopted. For instance, the Native American word *Wikiwahmi* is now *wigwam.* Many other words in use in the United States have come from other cultures.

The English language in the United States is constantly changing. As people learn that communication is possible only when the meaning of words is agreed upon, efforts are made to reach agreement. As people interact through communication, their separate cultures merge into a common culture.

United States culture now includes holidays and holy days from different countries. Foods

Changes in technology have created changes in lifestyles.

from other lands have become part of the United States diet. Styles of homes have also changed.

Technology helps people to have more material comforts, more conveniences, and more leisure time. A country's level of technology is based on the kind of machinery and skills used in that society. Each time a new tool or machine is developed, the culture changes. The change may be significant or only minor.

Structural change. Rural communities are characterized by extended families and interpersonal relationships with community members. The change from rural to urban living has resulted in a change in the family. Urban families usually consist of two parents (or often a single parent) and their children. Grandparents are located away from the nuclear family. When brothers and sisters become wage earners, they also leave the home of the nuclear family.

City dwellers often feel isolated from their neighbors. Ethnic communities within cities provide the close-knit relationships between neighbors so necessary for the psychological needs of people. Suburbs have also been formed giving people from the same social class a place to share mutual concerns and goals.

Complete these statements.

2.111 A society tends to be held together by a shared ____________________ .

2.112 Tensions and anxieties in society tend to be caused by sudden cultural ____________________ .

2.113 The most important component of culture is ____________________ .

Write *true* or *false*.

2.114 __________ The English language has remained unchanged since the translation of the King James Bible.

2.115 __________ Each time a new tool or machine is developed, some change takes place in culture.

Complete this activity.

2.116 Cite examples of cultural change brought about by a shift from rural to urban living.

____

____

____

____

____

____

____

____

Review the material in this section in preparation for the Self Test. This Self Test will check your mastery of this particular section as well as your knowledge of the previous section.

SELF TEST 2

Match the following (each answer, 2 points).

2.01 _______ Adam and Eve
2.02 _______ Great Plains Indians
2.03 _______ Hebrews
2.04 _______ utopia
2.05 _______ Eskimo
2.06 _______ Mercator
2.07 _______ Africans
2.08 _______ Holy Scriptures
2.09 _______ equator
2.010 _______ positivists
2.012 _______ equinox
2.013 _______ acculturation
2.014 _______ assimilation
2.015 _______ reliefs

a. map projection
b. an idealized society
c. accept only the knowledge based on observed facts
d. imaginary circle around the middle of the earth
e. geographical features
f. occurs when two societies interact
g. "eater of raw meat"
h. a "melting pot" of cultures
i. developed a written language and a code of laws
j. stereotype of the North American Indian
k. immigrants from Ireland
l. one culture is taken over by a more dominant culture
m. Anglo-Saxon Protestants
n. contributed Old Testament literature
o. the shared ancestors of all people
p. best tool for socialization
q. came as slaves
r. nights are twelve hours long

Complete these statements (each answer, 3 points).

2.016 ______________________ remains may include pottery, tools, and bones.

2.017 The most important single component of culture is ______________________ .

2.018 The historian, the anthropologist, and the sociologist all must avoid being ______________________ which would result in a study that favors one side over another.

2.019 a. ______________________ is the study of man, and b. ______________________ is the study of the earth.

2.020 Many immigrants came to the United States for: a. ______________________ , b. ______________________ , and c. ______________________ reasons.

2.021 The characteristics of any people's culture are directly affected by their ______________________ .

2.022 The ______________________ tribes of the Northeast supported the English during the Revolutionary War.

2.023 a. ______________________ describes people who wander in small groups searching for food while b. ______________________ describes people who farm a plot of land until its fertility is depleted.

2.024 In anthropology, ______________________ is defined as following a formula for doing things that are beyond one's own personal power.

2.025 The size, style, and construction of a shelter will depend on the a. ______________________ and the b. ______________________ of the society.

Write the letter for the correct answer on each line (each answer, 2 points).

2.026 Dates assigned to earth and to its prehistoric remains are ______ .
a. constant b. predictable c. only estimates d. absolute

2.027 History began with ______ .
a. Adam and Eve b. God the Father c. the Vikings d. Columbus

2.028 To do fieldwork, an anthropologist must ______ .
a. bring many gifts to trade
b. live among the people at least a year
c. write textbooks
d. form his opinion ahead of time

2.029 The sociologist is *primarily* concerned with the study of man's ______ .
a. social institutions
b. past events
c. physical characteristics
d. art and architecture

2.030 Native Americans may have come across the Bering Strait from ______ .

a. the Marquesas Islands
b. Europe
c. Africa
d. Asia

2.031 Anthropologists classify small, nonliterate societies by ______ .

a. language
b. how they obtain food
c. leadership styles
d. organization of families

2.032 A form of prejudice that keeps us from seeing people as individuals is called ______ .

a. divination
b. pluralism
c. positivism
d. stereotyping

2.033 Pastoral societies are usually ______ .

a. nomadic
b. stationary
c. unstable
d. complex

Write *true* or *false* (each answer, 1 point).

2.034 __________ The essential nature of man has remained unchanged since Adam.

2.035 __________ The ancient Hebrews believed that history had a beginning and an end.

2.036 __________ To fully understand the history of any civilization, you need only study that one civilization.

2.037 __________ Sudden cultural changes tend to cause tensions and anxieties.

2.038 __________ Philosophers long ago thought about an ideal society, but the science of sociology is relatively new.

2.039 __________ The ethnographer is not concerned with kinship or family relations.

2.040 __________ The language of the group being studied reveals how the group relates to the world.

2.041 __________ Concluding that a foreign culture is inferior to one's own is ethnocentrism.

2.042 __________ "Noble savage" refers to a member of the Five Civilized Tribes.

2.043 __________ A shift from country to city living seldom results in cultural change.

81/101 **SCORE** __________ **TEACHER** __________ __________
initials date

3. ECONOMICS AND POLITICS

Economics is the study of wealth. Economics deals with the choices people make between what they want and what is available. The basic needs of people everywhere are food, clothing, and shelter. The Bible teaches Christians that our heavenly Father knows all our needs.

Through the years people devised various economic systems to meet their needs. In this section of the LIFEPAC, you will learn about three methods of production and distribution of goods: **free enterprise**, communism, and socialism. Money is important in all civilized societies. You will learn that the Bible teaches us many principles of financial responsibility.

Political science is concerned with the rules and procedures man uses to govern himself. The roots of Western political thought have come from Jewish and Greek civilizations and from Christianity. In this section you will see how Western political thought directly influenced one of our nation's most important documents, the Preamble to the Declaration of Independence. You will learn to define important political and economic terms and to describe the political structure of the federal and state governments.

SECTION OBJECTIVES

Review these objectives. When you have completed this section, you should be able to:

9. Describe different economic systems.
10. Explain the origin of Western political thought.
11. Define important political and economic concepts.
12. Describe the political structure of the federal and state governments.

VOCABULARY

Study these words to enhance your learning success in this section.

agrarian (u grãr' ē un). Agricultural.

bicameral (bī kam' ur ul). Having two legislative houses.

candidate (kan' du dāt). A person who seeks, or is proposed for, some office.

capital (kap' u tul). Money or goods used to produce other goods.

competition (kom' pu tish' un). Economic rivalry among producers for the consumer's dollars.

confederacy (kun fed' ur u sē). An association of states or nations for a common purpose.

consumer (kun süm' ur). Person who uses food, clothing, or anything grown or made by producers.

empiricism (em pir' u siz um). Knowledge based on the physical senses of observation and experiment.

entrepreneur (än' tru pru nėr'). Person who organizes and manages a business or industrial enterprise.

equitable (ek' wu tu bul). Fair or just.

fideism (fēd' ā iz' um). Knowledge based on faith.

free enterprise (frē en′ tur prīz). Freedom of private business to operate competitively for profit without interference by the government.

hierarchy (hi′ u rär′ kē). Organization having higher and lower ranks.

interposition (īn′ tur pu zish′ un). Theory that a state may block enforcement of a federal law.

investment (in vest′ munt). Spending money to earn money.

lobbyist (lob′ ē ist). A person who tries to influence legislation.

mass produce (mas pru düs′). To make goods in large quantities by machinery.

nullification (nul′ u fu′ kā shun). Theory that a state may declare a federal law null and void or without force.

oligarchy (ol′ u gär′ kē). Form of government in which a few people have power.

platform (plat′ fôrm). Plan of action or statement of principles of a group.

political machine (pu lit′ u kul mu shēn′). Group of people controlling a political organization or party.

pragmatism (prag′ mu tiz um). Philosophy that what is practical ("whatever works") must be right and true.

rationalism (rash′ un ul iz′ em). Knowledge based on logical thinking.

secession (si sesh′ un). Theory that states have the right to leave the Union.

sovereign (sov′ run). Independent of the control of other governments.

specialization (spesh′ ul u zā shun). Craftsmen confine their work to the production of specific parts, goods, or commodities.

states' rights (stāts rīts). Powers belonging to the separate states under the United States Constitution.

tax (taks). A charge placed on a person, product, or corporation by the government.

unicameral (yü′ nu kam′ ur ul). Having only one house in the legislative body.

veto (vē′ tō). The right of a president or governor to reject bills passed by the legislature.

THE DISCIPLINE OF ECONOMICS

Economics is the study of the production, distribution, and consumption of wealth. It deals with the choices people make between what they want and what resources are available. Economists use many tools and methods in their work. They are interested in money, **competition**, the market, and government.

Wants and needs. Human wants are limitless and varied. People always seem to want more food, clothes, houses, cars, recreation, services, and so on. Human needs are more basic: food, clothes, and shelter. Matthew 6:31–33 teaches that our heavenly Father knows what we need and will provide these things.

People in the United States have been blessed with much more than their needs require. Even the poorest people in this country earn more money than three-fourths of the rest of the people in the world.

Most people in the underdeveloped countries of the world support themselves by farming. They have few tools and limited skills. The money they earn is spent on just keeping themselves alive. If they do not have an adequate crop and their relatives and neighbors cannot help them, they will probably starve.

People in simple societies depend on their own family efforts to supply their needs. Those people in complex societies depend on other people, such as farmers, processors, transporters, and grocers, to supply their needs. An **agrarian** society has characteristics of both a simple society and a complex society.

Available resources. A resource is something that a person uses to satisfy a need or want. Natural resources are those materials found in nature that man puts to his use. Human resources are all the people in society who work. Man-made resources are those **capital** goods that are used in the production of other goods.

All resources are limited; however, human wants are unlimited. As a result, many resources have been overused and in some cases severely depleted. A wise person will investigate alternative resources and alternative uses of resources.

Production problems. Many problems arise in production in a **free enterprise system**. One problem is obtaining the people to work at the jobs that need to be done. Assigning a wage to a particular job is a difficult task. The **consumer** indirectly determines the value of the job by deciding whether to pay for the product of that job.

Another problem exists in getting the right things produced in the right amounts. Again, the consumer determines what will be produced by what he is willing to buy. The amounts to be produced are determined by the incomes of the consumer. Fewer luxury items are produced because fewer people can afford them. As the demand for a product increases, the supply will also be increased by the producer. When the demand is greater than the supply, prices and profits generally rise. When the supply exceeds the demand, prices generally fall.

| Mass Production

Entrepreneurs are businessmen who manage production. They raise the money to start a business and to keep it going. They also choose the means of production that will bring the largest profit.

Production methods. Division of labor means that one person does a small portion of work on a large project. This procedure has proved to be a very efficient way to **mass produce** items. One industry that uses this method is the automobile industry.

Individuals, businesses, and geographical regions specialize in producing different products. **Specialization** allows more work to be done more efficiently. Products are better and more economical because the parts of a job are done by the workers, businesses, or areas best able to do the tasks.

Specialization increases trade. Products from one area are traded for products from other areas. Because of their specialization, individuals, regions, and countries become interdependent.

Complete the crossword.

3.1 ACROSS

1. Freedom of private business to operate competitively for profit without government interference.
2. Agricultural
3. An association of states or nations for a common purpose.
4. Economic rivalry among producers for the consumer's dollars.
5. Money or goods used to produce other goods.

DOWN

2. Knowledge based on the physical senses of observation and experiment.
3. A person who seeks, or is proposed for, some office.
4. Fair or just.
5. Philosophy that what is practical ("whatever works") must be right and true.
6. Having two legislative houses.
7. Knowledge based on faith.
8. Person who uses food, clothing, or anything grown or made by producers.
9. Person who organizes and manages a business or industrial enterprise.
10. Organization having higher and lower ranks.

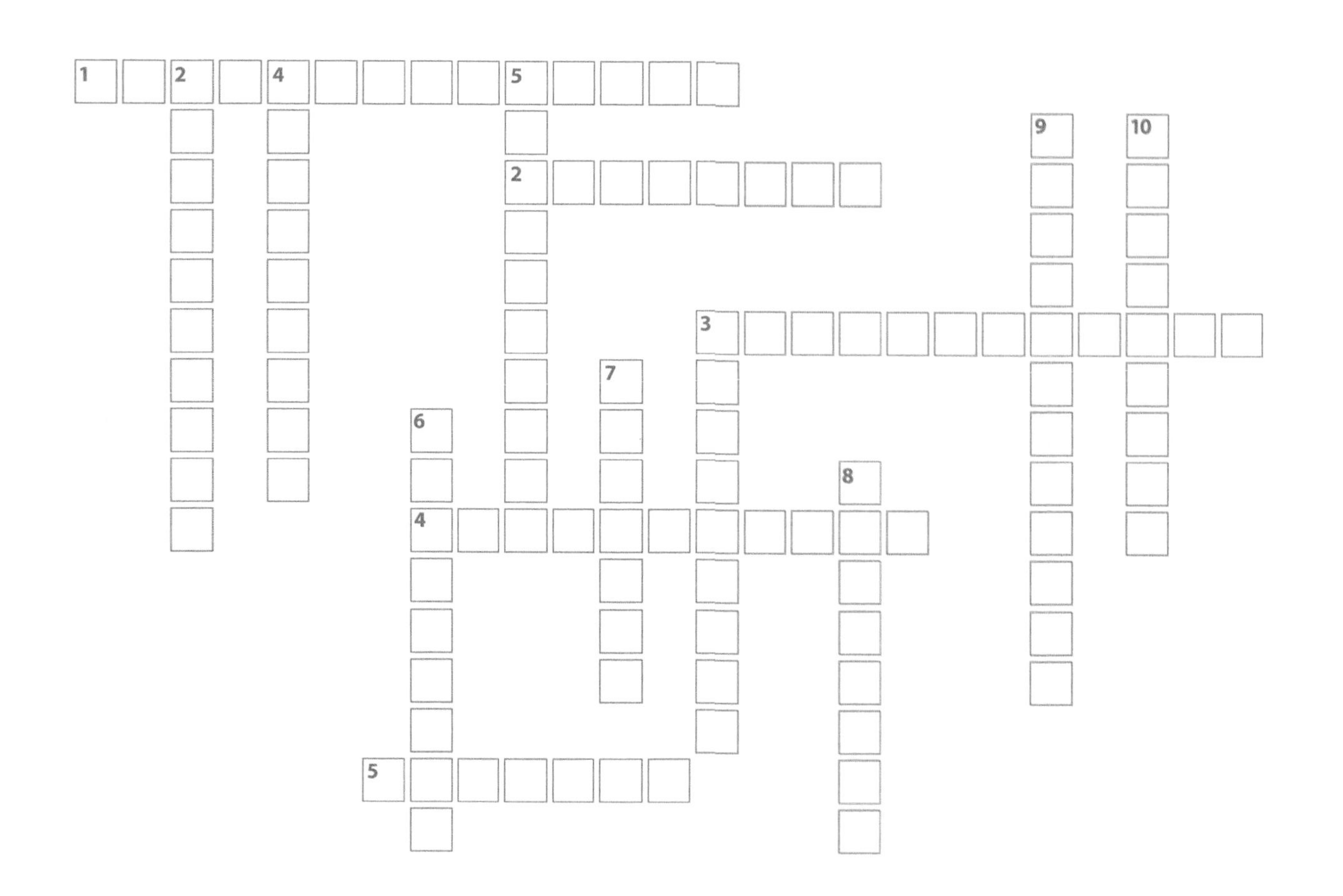

Match these terms with their definitions.

3.2 ______ rationalism
3.3 ______ secession
3.4 ______ sovereign
3.5 ______ specialization
3.6 ______ states' rights
3.7 ______ tax
3.8 ______ unicameral
3.9 ______ veto

a. craftsmen confining their work to the production of specific parts, goods, or commodities
b. the right of a president or governor to reject bills passed by the legislature
c. knowledge based on logical thinking
d. having only one house in the legislative body
e. theory that states have the right to leave the Union
f. a charge placed on a person, product, or corporation by the government
g. independent of the control of other governments
h. powers belonging to the separate states under the United States

Match these terms with their definitions.

3.10 ______ interposition
3.11 ______ investment
3.12 ______ lobbyist
3.13 ______ mass produce
3.14 ______ nullification
3.15 ______ oligarchy
3.16 ______ platform
3.17 ______ political machine

a. group of people controlling a political organization or party
b. theory that a state may block enforcement of a federal law
c. plan of action or statement of principles of a group
d. spending money to earn money
e. form of government in which a few people have power
f. a person who tries to influence legislation
g. theory that a state may declare a federal law null and void or without force
h. to make goods in large quantities by machinery

Complete these activities.

3.18 List four items in which economists are interested.

a. ______________________ b. ______________________

c. ______________________ d. ______________________

3.19 Economics is "the study of the a. ______________________,

b. ______________________, and c. ______________________ of wealth."

3.20 Basic human needs are for a. ______________________, b. ______________________,

and c. ______________________.

3.21 Most people in underdeveloped countries of the world support themselves

by ______________________.

3.22 Societies in which people depend on their family to supply their needs are called

______________________ societies.

3.23 Societies in which people depend on other people to supply their needs are called

______________________ societies.

Match these terms with their definitions.

3.24 ________ resource

3.25 ________ natural resources

3.26 ________ human resources

3.27 ________ capital

3.28 ________ free enterprise

3.29 ________ division of labor

3.30 ________ mass production

3.31 ________ specialization

a. used to satisfy a need or want

b. craftsmen working on specific goods or commodities

c. materials in nature that man uses

d. goods produced in large quantity

e. people in society who work

f. person does a smaller part or the larger project

g. money or goods used to produce goods

h. economic system based on competition and profit

Competition. Competition is economic rivalry among producers for the consumer's dollars. Producers compete by lowering prices to the lowest level possible that will still cover the cost of production and provide a reasonable profit. Competition of this kind results in a consumer's market: low prices benefit the consumer. Producers who do not make efficient use of their resources and who cannot adjust their prices to meet the competition will be forced to stop production.

When competition between producers is lacking and the demand for a product is high, prices will rise. This situation results in a producer's market: high prices will benefit the producers. Companies will realize a large profit.

Competition does not exist in a communist economic system. People are not allowed to employ others for any kind of profit-making business. The government makes all production decisions concerning the kind, quantity, and price of goods to be produced. The government also controls wages paid to workers. This government control provides little incentive to work hard and to do a good job.

In a communist system the government owns all natural resources, industry, banks, mass transportation, media, state farms, wholesale stores, and most retail stores. In a socialist system the government owns some things, such as railroads and heavy industries. Because some industries in socialist countries are owned by private citizens, supply and demand help to control prices.

Money. Money has three functions. It is a medium of exchange, having replaced bartering. It is a measure of value that helps a person to make comparisons of various goods and services. It also serves as a store of value.

Money can be created through a bank loan to a customer. The amount of money that can be created, however, is limited by the reserves of the bank. Money that is deposited in a financial institution can be loaned to entrepreneurs so that they can invest it in business. **Investment** means spending money on capital goods.

Education is also an investment. It improves the quality of labor and increases productivity. It also leads to technical progress.

The Bible has much to teach concerning financial matters. It teaches that God created all that exists and that He can easily supply us with what we need. Philippians 4:19 states, "But my God shall supply all your need according to his riches in glory by Christ Jesus." We are responsible to manage well the resources God gives us.

Good money management is accomplished through a personal financial program. One important Biblical principle of a financial program is to live without debt. Romans 13:8 states, "Owe no man anything..." To live without debt requires that one establishes reasonable economic goals.

Economic goals include immediate, intermediate, and long-range goals. To attain these goals, one needs resources, or income. The amount of income should equal the amount that one saves and spends to meet his goals. If the two amounts are not equal, one must either change his income or change his goals.

Goals

Immediate	Intermediate	Long Range
soda after school 50¢	roller blades $50.00	savings for car $1,000
card for grandma $2.00	mountain bike $125.00	
lunch $2.50	gym shoes $75.00	
	Christmas gifts $25.00	

Write *true* or *false*.

3.32 ____________ Competition is economic rivalry among producers for the consumer's dollars.

3.33 ____________ When producers raise their prices to the highest possible level, the result is a consumer's market.

3.34 ____________ Producers who cannot meet their competition will be forced to stop production.

3.35 ____________ When competition between producers is lacking, prices will rise and companies will make a large profit.

3.36 ____________ Communist economic systems do not allow profit-making businesses.

Complete these activities.

3.37 Explain the main differences between these two economic systems.

a. communist ____

____

____

b. socialist ____

____

____

3.38 List the three functions of money.

a. ____

b. ____

c. ____

3.39 The Bible encourages us to a. ____________________ well the resources God gives us and to avoid going into b. ____________________ .

THE ECONOMICS OF THE STATE

Each state has many financial responsibilities. States finance certain projects, pay salaries for state employees, pay state debts, and spend money in many other ways. To obtain the money they need, states collect **taxes** and borrow the necessary funds. Most of the funds states use come from federal grants.

Spending. State spending varies with the size of the state and the size of its government. State governments have grown recently through state aid to welfare and through increases in regulatory agencies. Total state spending is also influenced by inflation. Because inflation results in higher prices, the governor must periodically raise the state's budget. The major expense of state government is education. State governments are involved in many areas of research and public services. The legislature designates the funds spent by the state.

Taxing. A tax is a charge placed on an individual or a corporation by the government. Taxes must be paid. Governmental authority to tax comes from God. Romans 13:6 states "For this cause pay ye tribute also: For they are God's ministers, attending continually upon this very thing." The word *tribute* in this passage means *taxes*.

Many kinds of taxes are collected by a state. Property taxes are charged on the assessed value of a piece of property. Recently, state and local governments have raised property taxes. They have also raised assessed valuations to make them more equal to market values.

Many local school systems are funded by property taxes; however, they are not all funded equally. In a poor area where property values are low, school tax revenues are consequently low. In a rich area the property tax revenues are relatively high.

Income taxes are charged on the money earned by people or corporations. State income tax from an individual is normally a progressive tax: the rate of taxation increases as income increases. The tax rate for corporations is usually a flat rate.

Sales taxes are charged on the selling price of merchandise. Because of the possible inequities to the poor, many states do not charge sales taxes on such necessities as groceries and prescription drugs. Many states also do not tax such services as banks and dentists.

Other taxes include excise taxes, license fees, franchise taxes, inheritance taxes, estate taxes, and severance taxes.

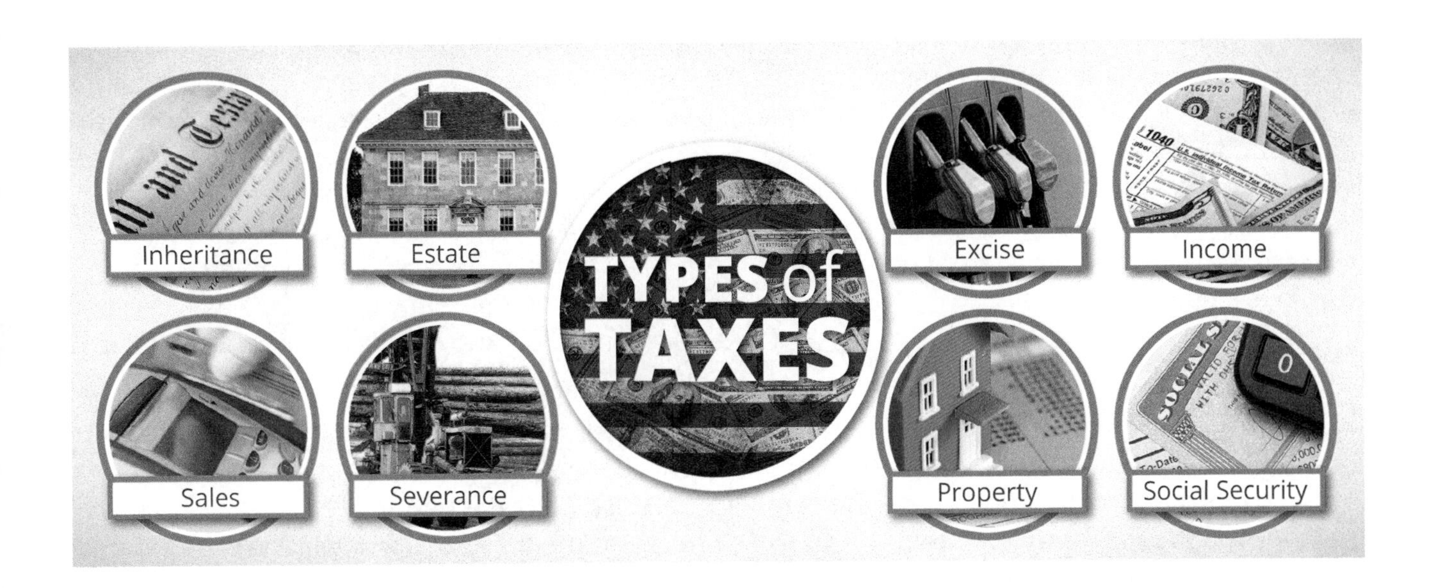

Taxes have risen sharply in the twentieth century. Much of the tax burden is placed on individuals. The burden of a tax is termed its incidence.

Borrowing. Increased spending has led some states to borrow money. States can obtain funds by issuing several types of bonds. States can also obtain short-term loans through banks, tax anticipation warrants, and other notes.

Complete these activities.

3.40 A ____________ is a charge placed on an individual, corporation, or product by the governor.

3.41 What is the major expense of state government? ______________________

3.42 State funds must be designated by the ______________________________ .

3.43 Beside each item below, give the name for a tax on the item.

a. assessed value of real estate: ______________________ tax

b. personal wages: ______________________ tax

c. selling price of merchandise: ______________________ tax

THE DISCIPLINE OF POLITICAL SCIENCE

Political science is concerned with the rules and procedures man uses to govern himself. The process of making rules and putting them into practice in society is called politics.

Political science can be divided into these categories: political theory, comparative government, and epistemology. Political theory is concerned with how man forms and views his governments. A political theorist may want to know where government leaders obtain their power and what political alternatives exist within a group.

Comparative government is the study of the ways in which governments work. It includes the descriptions of the political process in various nations and how nations interact. Comparative government also is concerned with comparing various governments of the world.

Epistemology means how we know what we know. Political scientists want to understand the basis for the political opinions of people.

Ways of knowing. People can know things by **empiricism**, by **rationalism**, and by **fideism**. Empiricism is knowing based on the physical senses. Our sense experiences provide us with most of the knowledge we use in daily life. However, we can be tricked by our senses to believe what is not really so. Oftentimes, if we had all of the facts concerning something, we would not be misled by our senses. Nevertheless, empirical knowledge alone is not sufficient to function adequately in the world.

Rationalism is knowing by logical thinking. Through rationalism we know something new because it fits the pattern of something we already knew. Rational knowledge is based on rational or logical patterns of thought. However, rational knowledge is only as reliable as the information upon which it is based. By itself, rationalism is not a sufficient base for knowledge.

Fideism is knowing through an act of faith. We can know by faith that God exists. We have not seen Him nor proved His existence through rational means, but as the Bible says (Hebrews 11:6), "...He that cometh to God must believe that he is...."

Our rational thoughts, our senses, and our faith work together in gaining knowledge. Using fideism as the only base for our knowledge about earthly things could be harmful. The appropriateness of an action done at the request of a person will be related to the integrity of that person. The Scriptures are the only true guide for life.

Complete these statements.

3.44 Political science is concerned with the rules and procedures man uses to ________________ himself.

3.45 Political theory is concerned with how man forms and views his ________________ .

3.46 Comparative government is the study of the ways in which different ________________ work.

3.47 Knowledge based on the physical senses is ________________ .

3.48 Knowledge based on logical thinking is ________________ .

3.49 Knowledge based on an act of faith is ________________ .

Write *true* or *false*.

3.50 ____________ Using any one way of knowing is sufficient in all areas of life.

3.51 ____________ The Holy Scriptures provide the only true guide for life.

Roots of Western political thought. From the time of the first written records, people have been selecting leaders, making rules, and discussing how society should be governed. Political thought has been a part of every civilization. The roots of Western political thought have come from three sources, including Jewish, Greek, and Roman civilizations.

Jewish civilization was formed under the leadership of Moses and under the direction of the Law of God. Moses led the people of Israel out of Egypt and away from the rules under which they had lived for more than four hundred years. The Israelites wandered for forty years in a barren wilderness. To settle the disputes of the people, Moses constructed a loose political organization. He judged only the most serious disputes, and a **hierarchy** of men judged disputes at the lower levels.

The Law of God was given to the Israelites through Moses. It included rules for man's relationship to the nation and for his relationships with his leaders and fellow man. Because the Law came from God, it would be unchangeable and unchanging. The Law was the first set of moral rules to be considered valid for all nations. It bound all men into a brotherhood of responsibility. Whatever the particular governmental structure or geographical location, the Law would remain active and binding.

Greek civilization was formed from small kingdoms called city-states. Each of the city-states was ruled by a king who was advised by influential warriors and citizens. In the Peloponnesian peninsula the king's advisors took the rulership and formed an **oligarchy**, the rule by a few.

The city of Athens had a form of democracy where leaders were elected by all male citizens. The constitution required every citizen to participate in government because his duty was to help the state in all things. However, no feeling for individual rights existed in Athens.

The first political science book was *The Republic*, written by Plato of Athens. Although the book describes the ideal form of government, its importance lies in asking questions about government. For the first time in Western civilization, government was seen as being man-made.

| Moses

Plato was interested in the ideal state, but his student Aristotle was interested in how things were in reality. In his book, *The Politics*, Aristotle classified governments into three classes: rule by one, rule by a few, and rule by many. His classification is still used in modern political science.

Important political ideas came from Athens. Aristotle stressed that the rule of good laws, rather than the rule of good men, makes good government. Plato said that men could correct the evils of government through systematic thought. The democracy of Athens showed that the ordinary person was capable of participating in government.

The Greeks and the Romans had similar beginnings but developed different forms of government. In contrast to the Greek democracy, the Romans had a representative form of government, a republic. The Roman Republic lasted for almost five hundred years and was then replaced by the Roman Empire.

During the time of Augustine (early fifth century after Christ), the Roman Empire was in upheaval and was facing collapse. The city of Rome was sacked in AD 410. Some Christians feared that the fall of the Roman government would mean the fall of Christianity. Augustine tried to dispel these fears in his work, *The City of God*.

Augustine had a linear view of history. History was not cyclical but was a line of man's development from Creation to the Judgment. Along that line lay two cities: The City of God and the earthly city. The City of God is governed by the rules of God and will never be destroyed. It is where the spirit of man lives. The earthly city could only be an imperfect copy of the City of

God. It is where all the matters of living as a human occur.

Augustine said that the basis of nations was sinful, being the domination of one man over others. Those nations that based their laws on the laws of God (laws of the City of God) were to be obeyed. Christians were to try to create on earth as much of the natural order in the City of God as possible. Treating all people as neighbors, justice, was one of the best reflections of the City of God.

| Aristotle

Thomas Aquinas gave his views of human government is his book, *Summa Theologica*. He said that three types of law exist. Divine law, the Word of God, was the highest law possible and had to be obeyed. Natural law was the feeling inside a person to discern between good and evil. Human law was the rules that told men how to act within a society that was always changing.

Aquinas said that the state only had control over the physical being of man. No man rules the soul of another, the place where true liberty is found. Although man must have government to solve earthly conflicts, Aquinas believed that rulers might use human laws to confuse feelings of good and evil. If people are confused about natural law, the state could carry out evil plans.

Complete this activity.

3.52 The roots of Western political thought have come from three sources:

a. ____ ,

b. ____ , and

c. ____ .

Match the following.

3.53 ________ Moses
3.54 ________ city-states
3.55 ________ oligarchy
3.56 ________ Athens
3.57 ________ hierarchy
3.58 ________ divine law
3.59 ________ Plato
3.60 ________ Aristotle
3.61 ________ Romans
3.62 ________ Augustine
3.63 ________ Thomas Aquinas

a. the Word of God
b. *Summa Theologica*
c. passed the Law of God to the Israelites
d. *The City of God*
e. small kingdoms
f. developed a republican form of government
g. rule by a small group
h. *The Politics* (classified governments)
i. leaders were elected by all male citizens
j. *The Republic*
k. group of officials to judge disputes

Modern political science. The beginning of modern political science occurred during the Renaissance. Niccolo Machiavelli was the first political scientist to use the empirical method. He wrote about what he observed rather than what he thought was ideal. His book, *The Prince*, argued that the basis of the state and of the ruler's authority was power. Rulers could use any means to gain power; they were not bound by morality.

Like Machiavelli, Thomas Hobbes lived during a time of social unrest. He wrote a book, *Leviathan*, describing the rise of the state (leviathan: giant) out of the state of nature. The state of nature was characterized by the absence of government or laws, absolute individual liberty, and constant warfare. The purpose of the state was to control the evil nature of man.

John Locke wrote *Two Treatises on Civil Government* in which he stressed the rights of man. Locke believed that man lived peacefully and according to natural law in the state of nature. Although all men were created equal, they banded together and formed nations to accomplish things that they could not do separately. Hence, no government can exist without the consent of the governed. The state was to protect the right of the citizen.

In his work, *The Essay on Liberty*, John Stuart Mill said that the freedom of any man is limited by the freedom his neighbor enjoys. The state is to protect the rights of the minorities from the power of a majority in a democracy.

The Declaration of Independence and the Constitution best show how the tradition of Western political thought was put into practice. Thomas Jefferson wrote the Declaration of Independence using many of the ideas and some of the exact words of John Locke. The preamble of this document contains five ideas from Western political thought:

1. God has granted equality to all men.
2. All men have equal rights at birth.
3. Human rights include life, liberty, and the pursuit of happiness.
4. Human rights are self-evident.
5. If a government abolishes human rights, the people can abolish that government.

Every person is raised within several environments: a social environment, a physical environment, and a political environment. The political environment is comprised of the religious and philosophical views of the majority in a group. The political environment is where beliefs about rule-making and politics occur.

Within the political environment is a decision-making organization. Aristotle said that only three forms of decision-making organizations exist: rule of one, rule of a few, and rule of many. If a group is too large for all to participate directly in government, the people can elect representatives to operate the government.

Requests of the government by the people are called inputs. *Demands* are inputs that ask the decision makers to do something; *supports* are inputs that tell the decision makers they did a good job.

Decisions made by a government are called *outputs. Rewards* are outputs that respond favorably to a demand. *Sanctions* are outputs that are punishments. *Symbols* are outputs that keep the citizens happy and aware that the rulers are listening to them.

The political process of all governments follows this cycle:

1. An event, problem, or thought occurs in the environment.

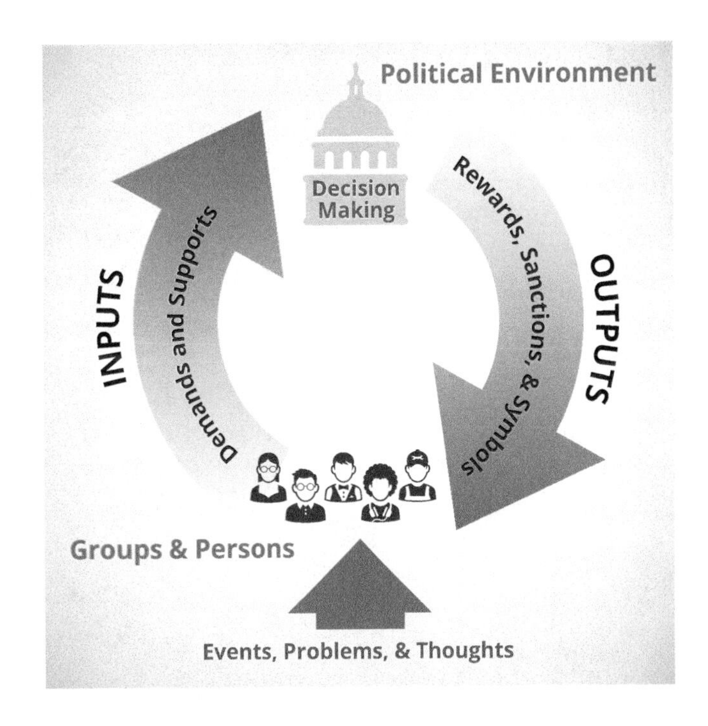

2. Citizens react to that event, problem, or thought.
3. Citizens form inputs to the government.
4. Government responds to the citizens through outputs.
5. Outputs lead to further inputs.

Political scientists make models of governments and politics. A model should be able to explain what is happening in the political environment and to predict what should occur in the future.

Write *true* or *false*.

3.64 ____________ Modern political science began with the Declaration of Independence.

3.65 ____________ Machiavelli was the first political scientist to use methods based on actual observation.

3.66 ____________ Machiavelli's book, *The Prince*, said rulers need not be bound by morality.

3.67 ____________ According to the *Leviathan* by Thomas Hobbes, the purpose of government was to control the evil nature of man.

3.68 ____________ The rights of man were stressed in *Two Treatises* on *Civil Government* by John Locke.

3.69 ____________ A man's freedom is unaffected by his neighbor's freedom, according to *The Essay on Liberty* by John Stuart Mill.

3.70 ____________ The two thinkers who most influenced Thomas Jefferson were Machiavelli and Hobbes.

Complete this activity.

3.71 What five vital ideas from Western political thought are contained in the Preamble of the Declaration of Independence?

a. ____

b. ____

c. ____

d. ____

e. ____

Complete these statements.

3.72 Federal authority is derived from the ______________ .

3.73 Both federal and state governments have three branches:

a. ______________________ , b. ______________________ , and

c. ______________________ .

Complete this activity.

3.74 Define these terms.

a. confederacy____

____

b. interposition ____

____

c. nullification ____

____

d. secession ____

____

THE GOVERNMENT OF THE STATE

State government existed before federal government. In fact, federal government is derived from state government. Both levels of government have the same structure: a legislative branch, an executive branch, and a judicial branch. Although some differences do occur, most state governments are basically the same.

Background. Thirteen independent **sovereign** states united in a **confederacy** to fight the British. Each state was really a separate country. The United States Constitution was drafted to strengthen the ties between the states.

Federal authority is conceived of as authority derived from the authority of the states. Some states have determined not to grant authority to the national government on certain occasions. Some states have used the principle of **interposition** in refusing to comply with federal law. Interposition means using state sovereignty to block enforcement of a federal law the state deems unconstitutional.

An extension of interposition is **nullification**. Nullification means that a state could declare a federal law null and void within its borders. Nullification was extended to the doctrine of **secession**: having the right to leave the Union if the Union violates the state's rights. The Civil War eliminated the doctrine of secession.

The state is a basic unit of government. Besides granting authority to the federal government, the state is the creator of all other levels of government. State governments pursue their own courses. Although **states' rights** are diminished, they still play a large role in shaping the United States system of government.

Structure. The structure of state government is like that of the federal government—it is divided into legislative, executive, and judicial branches. These three branches provide a system of checks and balances. This system was presented in Montesquieu's work, *Spirit of the Laws*.

Most state legislatures are **bicameral**, divided into two houses. The houses are usually called the House of Representatives and the Senate. Nebraska is **unicameral**, having only one house.

Some state legislatures have had problems with **equitable** representation. Usually, the rural population has been over-represented; and large, complex districts have been represented by at-large members. Some legislatures are almost totally dominated by one party. Each of these problems is beginning to change or is being corrected.

The average number of members in a House of Representatives (lower house) is about one hundred. They are presided over by a speaker of the house. The state Senate (upper house) is smaller than the lower house and is presided over by the lieutenant governor.

A bill goes through the following steps to become a law:

1. The bill is introduced, given a number, and assigned to a committee.
2. The committee considers the bill and sends it to the floor for debate and approval.
3. The bill is sent to the other house to a committee and onto the floor for debate and approval.
4. The bill goes to a joint committee to resolve house differences.
5. The bill goes back to both houses for approval, and then it is sent to the governor.
6. The governor signs the bill into law.
7. If the governor **vetoes** the bill, it becomes law by a two-thirds override vote of the legislature.

Some organizations keep full-time personnel at the state capital. These people are called **lobbyists** and represent the interests of their group before the legislature. Lobbyists most often represent special interest groups.

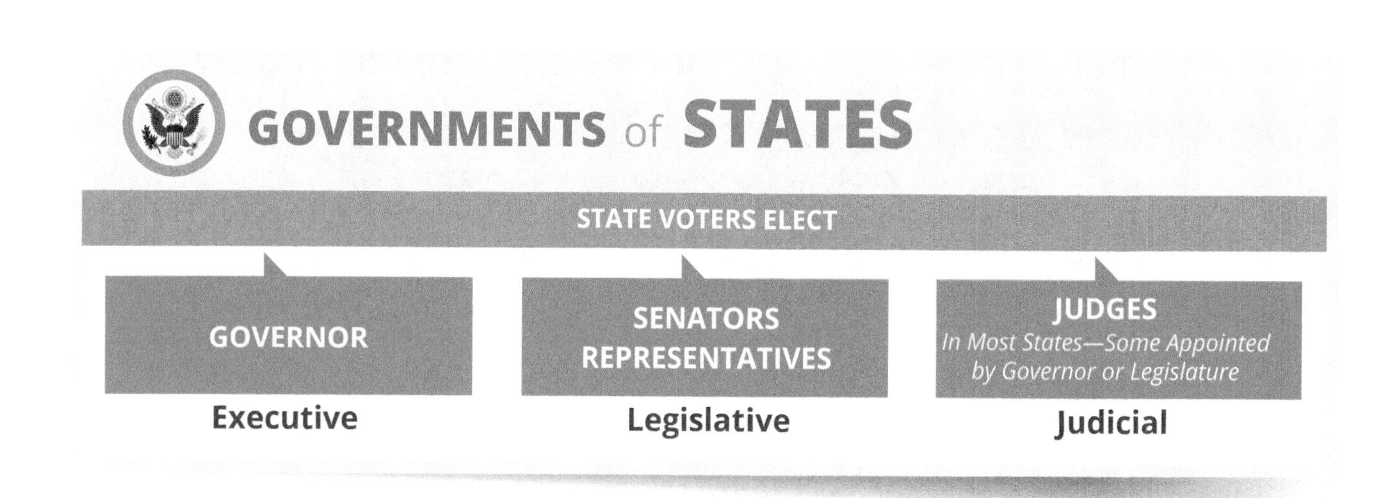

The executive branch of state government is headed by the governor. Governorships can be characterized as being either strong or weak. A strong governorship is one where the governor appoints his own cabinet; almost all of the state administrators report to him. A weak governorship is one where almost every major office-holder is elected. Elected officials have a sense or responsibility to the voters who elected them, rather than to the governor.

The argument for a strong governorship stresses that the concentration of power in the governor makes management of government more efficient. The argument for a weak governorship stresses that power concentrated in one person reduces individual freedom. Also, when executive departments and agencies are relatively independent, they act as a check-and-balance system to prevent abuse of power. Those states that spread executive power among several elected officials use a long ballot to list all the **candidates**.

All governors have similar responsibilities. They control the state police, the national guard, and civil defense efforts. They prepare the state budget and appoint judges and replacements to the unexpired terms of elected officials.

Governors can sign legislation into law or they can veto it. A governor is able to pardon a criminal or to commute a prisoner's sentence. Because of his position, a governor is usually the head of his political party.

Besides the governor, several important officials comprise the executive branch of state government. The lieutenant governor presides over the state Senate and completes the unexpired term of the governor if the governor leaves his office. The attorney general is the state's lawyer. His advice is particularly sought on matters involving the state's constitution. The Secretary of State, the state treasurer, the state auditor, the state superintendent of public instruction, and a host of regulatory agencies and commissions complete the executive branch. These executive agencies sometimes have quasi-legislative and quasi-judicial powers.

The judicial branch of state government is a court system divided into districts. District courts are often specialized, handling only criminal cases or only civil cases. The district attorney is the local prosecutor. Appeals from district courts are handled by that state Supreme Court. Appeals from the state Supreme Court go directly to the United States Supreme Court.

Complete these statements.

3.75 The three branches of government provide a system of a. ______________ and b. ______________ .

3.76 A legislature divided into two houses is a. ______________ ; a legislature having only one house is b. ______________ .

3.77 People who represent special interest groups before the legislature are ______________ .

 **Complete this activity.**

3.78 Define these terms.

a. strong governorship ____

____

____

b. weak governorship ____

____

____

Match the following.

3.79	________ House of Representatives	a.	court system
3.80	________ Senate	b.	unicameral
3.81	________ Nebraska	c.	lower house
3.82	________ executive branch	d.	upper house
3.83	________ judicial branch	e.	governor

THE POLITICS OF THE STATE

Politics in the United States are continually changing. New political parties have emerged since the colonial period. Political viewpoints and political power have also been influenced by changes in society. However, politics itself has not changed. It is still a game of power.

Political parties. A political party is a group of voters who share a similar political point of view. They support candidates who share the beliefs of the group. The United States has two major parties: Republican and Democratic. Several smaller parties are also active, such as the Libertarian Party and the American Independent Party.

Political parties in the United States reflect an English tradition. In the eighteenth century, England had two dominant parties: the Tories and the Whigs. The Tories were the party of the aristocracy; the Whigs were the party of the middle class industrialists. The colonists who remained loyal to England were called Tories, and those who joined the revolution were called Whigs.

One of the first political parties in the United States was the Federalist Party. It was focused on Alexander Hamilton's ideas of a strong central government and closer ties to England. A second party, the Democratic-Republicans, was focused on Thomas Jefferson's ideas of weak central government, states' rights, and closer ties to France. The Democratic-Republicans are now the Democratic Party.

The Whig Party was formed in 1832 from National Republicans, Democrats, and Federalists. Many northern Whigs joined the antislavery Republican Party in the late 1850s. Beginning in 1860 with Abraham Lincoln, the Republicans dominated the government until the election of Franklin Roosevelt in 1933. The Democrats then became the majority party until 1994 when the Republicans were again in the majority.

Democrats tend to favor increased federal spending, social legislation, and government involvement in the economy. Republicans tend to favor sound money, business interests, less international involvement, and less government.

Political parties are organized at the precinct, county, state, and national levels. Each level has a committee and a chairman. Each level also provides a **platform** and delegates to the party's conventions. A dissatisfied group within a party can hold a separate, or rump, convention.

Political viewpoints. Two major viewpoints in the United States are conservatism and liberalism. Conservatives originally favored royalty, the nobility, and the state-controlled churches. Conservatives today favor increased law and order and a stronger economy apart from government interference. Liberals originally supported individual and economic freedoms and less centralized authority. Liberals began supporting more progressive social legislation including government intervention in business.

A third political viewpoint is that of the moderates. They reflect a tradition of **pragmatism**. A Christian would have difficulty being a political pragmatist; he must make decisions based on God's Word rather than on whatever works.

Political power. Politics is a game of power. Power can be used for either good or evil ends. A **political machine** is a group of powerful people dedicated to keeping a certain group of candidates in office. Political machines include Tammany Hall and various families in the South. Labor unions, companies, and men of finance and of business are sources of wealth, and wealth is a source of political power.

Write *true* or *false*.

3.84 ____________ No new political parties have emerged in the United States since the colonial period.

3.85 ____________ Politics is a game of power.

3.86 ____________ Power can only be used for evil purposes.

3.87 ____________ A political machine is a group of people dedicated to keeping a certain group of candidates in office.

3.88 ____________ Wealth is a source of power.

Complete these statements.

3.89 A political ____________________ is a group of voters who share a similar point of view.

3.90 The United States has two major political parties: a. ____________________ and b. ____________________ .

3.91 Three political viewpoints in the United States are a. ____________________ , b. ____________________ , and c. ____________________ .

3.92 A Christian's political decisions must be based upon ____________________ Word.

Before you take this last Self Test, you may want to do one or more of these self checks.

1. _______ Read the objectives. See if you can do them.
2. _______ Restudy the material related to any objectives that you cannot do.
3. _______ Use the **SQ3R** study procedure to review the material:
   a. **S**can the sections.
   b. **Q**uestion yourself.
   c. **R**ead to answer your questions.
   d. **R**ecite the answers to yourself.
   e. **R**eview areas you did not understand.
4. _______ Review all vocabulary, activities, and Self Tests, writing a correct answer for every wrong answer.

SELF TEST 3

Match the following with their definitions (each answer, 2 points).

3.01 ________ anthropology
3.02 ________ acculturation
3.03 ________ physical geography
3.04 ________ economics
3.05 ________ fideism
3.06 ________ rationalism
3.07 ________ oligarchy
3.08 ________ history
3.09 ________ climatology
3.010 ________ assimilation
3.011 ________ competition
3.012 ________ sociology
3.013 ________ political science
3.014 ________ hierarchy
3.015 ________ meteorology

a. the study of man's past
b. one culture is taken over by a more dominant culture
c. the study of the production, distribution, and consumption of wealth
d. study of the earth's atmosphere
e. the rules and procedures man uses to govern himself
f. the study of average weather
g. the study of man's ways of life or culture
h. way of knowing based on logical thinking
i. government having higher and lower ranks
j. law of supply and demand
k. the study of features of the earth
l. economic rivalry among producers for the consumer's dollars
m. government by a small group of people
n. the study of man's social groups and institutions
o. way of knowing based on an act of faith
p. occurs when two societies interact by borrowing and trading cultures

Write the letter for the correct answer on each line (each answer, 2 points).

3.016 Most people in the underdeveloped countries of the world support themselves by ______ .
a. mass production b. free enterprise c. farming d. competition

3.017 Societies in which people depend on other people to supply their needs are called ______ .
a. primitive b. socialist c. communist d. complex

3.018 A consumer's market exists when ______ .
a. prices are lowest
b. prices are highest
c. production stops
d. competition is lacking

3.019 The investment of capital usually depends upon the use of ______ .
a. natural resources
b. human resources
c. money resources
d. governmental resources

3.020 Geographical features, such as mountains, plains, and oceans, are ______ .
a. spherical b. reliefs c. contiguous d. linear

3.021 Dates assigned to earth and to its prehistoric remains are ______ .
a. scientifically proved
b. only estimates
c. predictable
d. constant

3.022 History begins with ______ .
a. the scattering of people from the city of Babel
b. the crossing of the Bering Straits by native Americans
c. the discovery of the New World
d. God the Father before Creation

3.023 To do fieldwork, an anthropologist must ______ .
a. live among the people at least one year
b. bring a supply of trade goods
c. help the natives devise a written language
d. know ahead of time the social conditions he will find

3.024 The shape of the earth is ______ .
a. a perfect sphere
b. a revolving cone
c. an imperfect sphere
d. a flat, smooth mass

Complete these statements (each answer, 3 points).

3.025 *Mercator*, *polar*, and *interrupted area* are names given to three important ______________ projections.

3.026 The characteristics of any people's culture, or way of life, are directly affected by their ______________ .

3.027 The most important single component of culture is ______________ .

3.028 Many immigrants came to the United States seeking a. ______________ , b. ______________ , or c. ______________ freedom.

3.029 The three branches of government in the United States provide a system of a. ______________ and b. ______________ .

Write *true* or *false* (each answer, 1 point).

3.030 __________ The governor must sign into law all bills passed by both houses of the legislature.

3.031 __________ Most state legislatures are bicameral.

3.032 __________ States may raise money by issuing checks and balances.

3.033 __________ A tax is a charge placed on an individual, product, or corporation by the government.

3.034 __________ A lobbyist represents a special interest group before the legislature.

3.035 __________ The Bible teaches that our heavenly Father knows all human needs.

3.036 __________ The communistic economic system encourages private investment, competition, and profit.

3.037 __________ When the supply of a commodity exceeds the demand, prices generally fall.

3.038 __________ Man everywhere is engaged in spiritual, human, and natural areas of conflict.

3.039 __________ The earth makes one complete rotation every twenty-four hours.

3.040 __________ The science of sociology is primarily concerned with trying to create an ideal society.

3.041 __________ Family relations and kinship patterns provide valuable data for the ethnographer.

3.042 __________ A shift from rural to urban living does much to relieve social tensions and hostilities.

3.043 __________ Most citizens of the United States are immigrants, or the descendants of immigrants.

3.044 __________ Facial features, skin color, and hair texture are among the noticeable areas of racial difference.

3.045 __________ The life of the Eskimo is an example of the adaptation of culture to environment.

3.046 __________ Regional landforms found in North America had no effect upon the culture of the Indians or the early settlers.

Put these events in the proper order: first, second, third, and so on (each answer, 2 points).

3.047 _______ The bill goes to a joint committee to resolve differences.

3.048 _______ The governor may veto the bill or sign it into law.

3.049 _______ The committee considers the bill and sends it to the floor for debate and approval.

3.050 _______ The bill goes back to both houses for approval and then is sent to the governor.

3.051 _______ The bill is introduced, given a number, and assigned to a committee.

3.052 _______ The bill is sent to the other house to a committee and onto the floor for debate and approval.

3.053 _______ If the governor vetoes the bill, the legislature may override the veto by a two-thirds vote.

82/103 **SCORE** __________ **TEACHER** __________ __________

initials date

Before taking the LIFEPAC Test, you may want to do one or more of these self checks.

1. ________ Read the objectives. See if you can do them.
2. ________ Restudy the material related to any objectives that you cannot do.
3. ________ Use the **SQ3R** study procedure to review the material.
4. ________ Review activities, Self Tests, and LIFEPAC vocabulary words.
5. ________ Restudy areas of weakness indicated by the last Self Test.

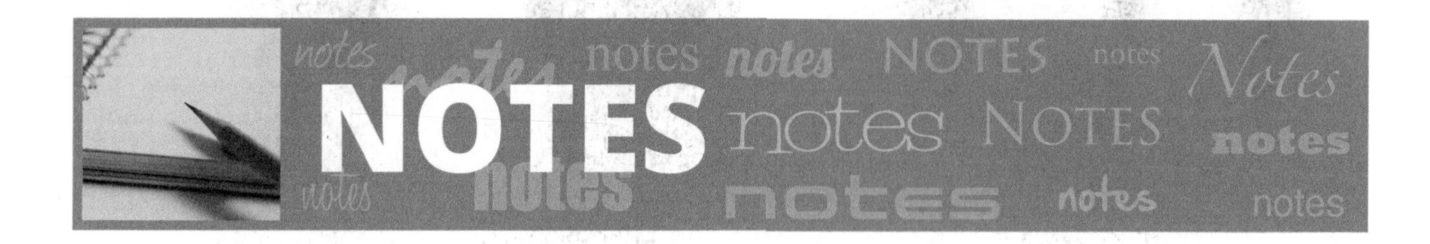
notes
notes
notes
NOTES
notes
Notes
NOTES
notes
NOTES
notes
notes
notes
notes
notes
notes